MY SONG

Sande Schones

WESTBOW
PRESS®
A DIVISION OF THOMAS NELSON
& ZONDERVAN

WestBow Press books may be ordered through booksellers or by contacting:

WestBow Press
A Division of Thomas Nelson & Zondervan
1663 Liberty Drive
Bloomington, IN 47403
www.westbowpress.com
1 (866) 928-1240

ISBN: 978-1-5127-9821-0 (sc)
ISBN: 978-1-5127-9823-4 (hc)
ISBN: 978-1-5127-9822-7 (e)

Library of Congress Control Number: 2017912477

Print information available on the last page.

WestBow Press rev. date: 08/17/2017

Dedicated to

JESUS

THE GREAT PHYSICIAN

Contents

Prologue

I was diagnosed with stage 4 cervical cancer in August of 2008. That diagnosis also included a rare cancer--stage IV Papillary Serous. Given a 20% chance of survival with 2 to 6 months to live devastated me beyond comprehension! However, my first line of defense was the word of God, with my prayer partners in strong support. Without hesitation, our multiple-denominational Bible study group gathered at a local church for prayer and intercession on my behalf. Our prayer time was sprinkled with tears and hope. Chris Watkins, our group leader, offered a powerful, prophetic prayer that I would live and not die, declaring that I had more songs to write and to sing. I've written and sung dozens of songs throughout the years, although I hadn't written or sung in some time; but, true to Chris' prophetic prayer, I have written and sung again. However, even without musical notes or rhyming lyrics, this book is truly My Song.

Introduction

Healing comes in many forms. My journey treading through the murky, treacherous, shark-infested waters of cancer is just that ... my journey. I do not expect anyone to have the exact results that I have had. I certainly do not believe in one formula for healing.

There are a myriad healings recorded in the scriptures. Jesus, however, did not heal everyone with the same method. Indeed, He did not even heal everyone! In Matthew's gospel we find these words, "So they were offended at Him. But Jesus said unto them, a prophet is not without honor, except in his own country and in his own house. NOW HE DID NOT DO MANY MIGHTY WORKS THERE BECAUSE OF THEIR UNBELIEF." (Matthew 13:57-58-NKJV)

The Apostle Paul asked three times to be healed from his infirmity. Jesus said to him, "My grace is sufficient for you, for my strength is made perfect in weakness." (II Corinthians 12:9) Jesus was telling Paul that he would be fully able to live with his infirmity by the grace of God.

Jesus said to the Roman Centurion, "Go your way and as you have believed so let it be done unto you." (Matthew 8:13) Jesus re-diagnosed the death of a young girl as "just sleeping". (Mark 5:39-42) Others, He literally raised from the dead. (John 11:43-44, Luke 7:14-15) To one, he applied the medicine of his spittle mixed with dirt to the eyes of a blind man. (John 9:6) Even after this unique application, the 'patient' did not see clearly, so Jesus reapplied the medicine with the result being a complete healing of the blind eyes. (I have much more to say about this particular miracle relating to my own healing, in a later chapter.)

I have mentioned a mere scattering of the miracles that Jesus performed, and only a few of His methods. The Bible records only about 40 miracles that Jesus performed during the three and a half years of His earthly ministry. The first recorded miracle was the famous turning of water into wine at the wedding feast. (John 2:1-11) Obviously, Jesus loves a good celebration!

The disciple, John, ended his gospel about the 'life and times of Jesus' with these words, "And there are also many other things that Jesus did, which if they were written one by one, I suppose that even the world itself could not contain the books that would be written. Amen." (John 21:25) Imagine that! John states that Jesus did so many miracles that there was not enough time and space to record them.

I highly recommend and strongly encourage everyone to read the four Gospels, written by Matthew (a converted tax collector), Mark (who accompanied Paul on his first missionary journey), Luke (a physician), and John (the young disciple who witnessed the crucifixion of Jesus). These writings are informative, exciting, dramatic, politically incorrect, historically accurate, daring, truthful, life altering, deliriously happy and tragically sorrowful, yet definitely triumphant.

What a read!

Purpose

My purpose in writing 'My Song' is to reveal Jesus for who He truly is--The Wonderful Counselor, The Mighty God, The Everlasting Father, and Prince of Peace. (Isaiah 9:6)

Mary, his mother, was told to name him Jesus, "For He shall save his people from their sins." The Greek dictionary defines "salvation" as meaning: rescue or safety, deliver, health, healing, save, etc.

Often when we hear the word "salvation" we think of a band of older men or women wearing army uniforms, ringing a bell and asking for money. We may think of it as some far-out religious term that has little meaning for us in today's society.

Jesus was sent to save us, to counsel us, and to be a Father to us. He also came bring healing and peace to our lives and bring us abundant life! Jesus said of Himself, "I AM THE WAY ... THE TRUTH ... THE LIFE." (John 14:6)

"I have come to give abundant life." (John 10:10)

THIS BEGS THE QUESTION ... WHO DOES NOT WANT LIFE?

I needed to be rescued from cancer. I needed to be delivered from fear. I needed health and hope; it all comes from Jesus. He is the saving of every situation, be it spiritual or physical.

I hope to encourage anyone facing a giant of any kind. Let it be said here and now, cancer is NOT a death sentence. Neither is any disease or malady known to man--you name it. It matters not. Jesus is the Way Maker and He can and will make a way for you and for me. It may not be the way we would think or orchestrate it; however, it is a better way. It is His way.

Cancer

(Jeremiah 8:20-22)

Jeremiah is known as the weeping prophet. His personal sorrow over the sinful state of his beloved Judah, and the many messages of God's impending judgment over the nation, caused this prophet unparalleled sorrow; hence, his lament is found in Jeremiah 8:20-22. "The harvest is past, the summer is ended, and we are not saved. For the hurt of the daughter of my people I am hurt; I am in mourning; astonishment has taken hold on me. Is there no balm in Gilead; is there no physician there? Why then is not the health of the daughter of my people restored?"

A footnote in the King James Study Bible records this: "Jeremiah is overcome with grief for his people. As the passing of a harvest season that failed to produce fruit gives rise to despair for the availability of food, so the passing days without repentance in Judah made destruction inevitable. Jeremiah was dismayed and cried out for relief for his people because of their sins, their wounds were incurable. Gilead was apparently known for its healing balm.

What does this have to do with cancer? Since having had cancer, I look at this disease as a formidable enemy, much as Jeremiah looked at the devastation of sin's toll on his people. As sin destroys lives, so also does cancer. When cancer strikes, it does not strike just the victim.

Cancer strikes the family, the friends, indeed, the whole community. We all know someone who has been diagnosed with this dreadful disease. The fear and tears that accompany that announcement are heart wrenching. According to the American Cancer Society (ACS), this year, about 1.5 million new cases of cancer are expected; tragically, more than half a million people are expected to die from this enemy. That is more than 1,500 people a day.

With all this research and billions of dollars spent trying to find a cure, why is there no cure? Breakthrough in cancer research comes in different forms. Some breakthrough is about prevention. This is positive. At least we can have some control. In 1954, for example, the link between smoking and lung cancer was discovered. In 2006, Gardasil was approved by the Food and Drug Administration as a vaccine for the prevention of cervical cancers. But we do not know what the final outcome of this drug will have in future years of those being treated. In fact, even now, some politicians, physicians, and previous supporters of Gardasil are backing off of its claims.

Other breakthroughs have to do with early detection. In 1960, the ACS began advocating pap smears for women, which led to a 70 percent decrease in deaths from cervical and uterine cancers. Chemotherapy and radiation has saved many lives, but in some instances, the cure is worse than the disease, contributing to the death of the patient.

With all this being said, I want to say that I THINK the chemo and radiation treatments that I had helped to save my life, but I KNOW that without the "balm of Gilead" in the hand of the Great Physician, Jesus, I would not have survived. Being given only several months to live and a 20 percent chance of survival, my future was definitely limited.

I thank God that there is 'balm' in Gilead, and that there is a Great Physician. The prophet Isaiah described Him, "He was wounded for our transgressions, bruised for our iniquities; the chastisement of our peace was upon Him; AND BY HIS STRIPES WE ARE HEALED." (Isaiah 53:5)

4

One of the Names of God is Jehovah-Rapha, meaning "The Lord Our Healer." The Bible tells us that Jesus came to heal. Hebrews 13:8 says, "He is the same, Yesterday, Today, Forever." Therefore, by faith I believe that Jesus heals today. He heals all manner of diseases.

John the Baptist, Jesus' cousin, was thrown into Herod's prison on a trumped up charge. When John began to hear of the miracles that Jesus was performing, he sent two of his disciples to ask Jesus, "Art thou He that should come, or do we look for another?" Jesus answered and said unto them, "Go and show John again those things which you do hear and see; the blind receive their sight and the lame walk, the lepers are cleansed and the deaf hear, the dead are raised up and the poor have the gospel preached to them." (Matthew 12:2-5-KJV)

Matthew records, "And great multitudes came unto Him having with them those that were lame, blind, dumb, maimed and many others, and cast them down at Jesus' feet and HE HEALED THEM. INASMUCH THAT THE MULTITUDE WONDERED, WHEN THEY SAW THE DUMB TO SPEAK, THE MAIMED TO BE WHOLE, THE LAME TO WALK, AND THE BLIND TO SEE, AND THEY GLORIFIED THE GOD OF ISRAEL." (Matthew 15:30-32)

Statistics

Statistics tell us that there are more heart related deaths in the United States than from any other cause of death, yet it is not heart attack, heart failure, or stroke that we fear the most, but that dreaded 'C' word--cancer. I faced both of these demon giants in 2008.

Rewind from 2008 back to 1955. I attended a country school in Covert, Kansas. We had a teacher for fifth through eighth grades, in one classroom. I'll call our teacher Miss Sharon (not her real name). We thought she was the meanest, strictest, most hateful teacher in the whole state of Kansas, if not in the whole United States; or, better yet, in the whole wide world! I was in the 7th grade. Miraculously, the following year, as an eighth grader, the school district hired a new teacher for our classroom--Miss Janette (not her real name; names are changed to protect the guilty). Well, no one on earth could be as bad, as mean, and as hateful as Miss Sharon, right? Wrong! Miss Janette was much, much worse. How could this happen?

I relate this bit of trivial information about Miss Sharon and Miss Janette to emphasize my experience with heart disease and cancer. Just when I thought it couldn't get worse, it did.

Fast forward to 2008. I'd just turned 65. I'd kept myself in good shape my whole life, or so I thought. I was only a few pounds overweight. I watched what I ate, going easy on bacon, red meat, and fried foods. Maybe my downfall was pastries? I took lots of vitamins and supplements. In fact, just days before I was rushed to a nearby hospital for an emergency triple by-pass, I was bragging to my friend, Rhonda, about a miraculous supplement that I was taking. It came with the promise that by adding this to your diet, you'd never be sick of anything! Well, so much for that false claim!

I prided myself on working out at 'Curves' several times a week. I spent countless hours combing the beach collecting agates. I'd park my truck, walk down to the beach, and spend several hours a day bending down on the soft sand hundreds of times, picking up these fabulous treasures.

I began to notice that when I walked back up the hill to my pick up, I was a little breathless. It concerned me, so I made an appointment with my doctor to do a treadmill test. I didn't exactly 'pass' the test, but I didn't fail it either. They described my test as a false positive, stating that it was inconclusive. Before I had a chance to follow it up with another test, I was, suddenly and without any further warning, awakened on the morning of April 8th (our youngest daughter's 35th birthday) with excruciating pain in my left arm and chest. Putting the planned birthday party 'on hold', I was rushed to our local hospital. Thanks to the quick thinking and action of Dr. Ashley Forsythe, an ambulance was ordered, and I was whisked fifty miles away to Good Samaritan Hospital in Corvallis, Oregon, where I underwent a triple by-pass to save my life.

For some reason, I was not afraid to die; that is, of this sudden heart event. HOWEVER, I was very frightened in the ambulance, as there had been an early spring snow and hail storm in the wee hours of that morning. Highway 20 is treacherous on a good day, let alone a day with black ice, without a hint of sunshine.

I looked out the ambulance windows onto the frozen hillsides, careening around the twists and turns of Highway 20. I began to wonder if I'd get to the hospital alive. I became very frightened, almost panicking as I visualized headlines in the local paper--PATIENT ON

THE WAY TO HEART SURGERY DIES IN ICY AMBULANCE
CRASH ON HIGHWAY 20.

Recently, our Bible Study group had been studying in the Old
Testament about the children of Israel. Oh, how they'd complained
against God! To punish them, God sent snakes among them. You
might be thinking, "HARSH", but I guess you could be thanking God
that now we live in a day of Grace.

Many died of snake bites, until Moses sought God on behalf of
the people. "So the Lord said to Moses, 'Make a snake and put it up on
a pole.' So Moses made a bronze snake and put it up on a pole. Then
when anyone was bitten by a snake and looked at the bronze snake,
he lived." (Numbers 21:8,9)

I looked up at the back windows of the ambulance and saw
the double entwined snakes on a pole (which, interestingly, is the
American Medical Association's symbol of health and healing).
Hmmm. I knew I would not die in an ambulance wreck. I figured
if it was good enough for Moses and God's people, then it was good
enough for me.

From that moment on, I was calm and serene. I had a supernatural
peace about me. After I arrived at Good Samaritan Hospital, I waited
in the ICU for my turn in the operating room. This calm, unearthly
peace was not the case when, six short months later, I was diagnosed
with stage 4 cancer.

Even though heart-related disease takes more people to their
grave than does cancer, it was cancer that put dread in my heart. This
was Miss Sharon compared to Miss Janette! Miss Sharon was a piece
of cake (to coin a phrase) compared to Miss Janette, and I knew I was
in for the battle of my life.

Trees

"And the Lord God commanded the man, saying, of every TREE of the garden you may freely eat; but of the tree of knowledge of good and evil, you shall not eat of it: for in the day that you eat thereof you shall surely die." (Genesis 2:16-17)

When Adam and Eve partook of the Tree of the Knowledge of Good and Evil, therefore disobeying the Creator, death entered the human race. ALL maladies of mankind are a result of that disobedience in the Garden of Eden, including cancer.

When my grandson, Elias, and I talk about this incident, he usually gets mad at Adam and Eve and expresses his anger and frustration, "This is all their fault!"

The Bible says, "It is appointed unto man once to die."

Now, I was facing death, diagnosed with an aggressive rare cancer, and I did not want to die. I was in league with Elias at this point. I was kind of mad at Adam and Eve. Couldn't they just have obeyed God and stayed away from that one tree? They'd been given everything. Was that too much to ask?

My very favorite poem is "Trees", by Joyce Kilmer, 1886-1918 American journalist, poet, literary lecturer, and editor. Though a prolific poet, whose works celebrated the common beauty of the natural world as well as his religious faith, Kilmer is remembered most for a poem entitled "Trees". The following poem is the original written by Kilmer:

Trees

By Joyce Kilmer

I think that I shall never see
A poem as lovely as a tree.
A tree whose hungry mouth is pressed
Against the earth's sweet flowing breast;
A tree that looks at God all day,
And lifts her leafy arms to pray;
A tree that may in Summer wear
A nest of robins in her hair;
Upon whose bosom snow has lain;
Who intimately lives with rain.
Poems are made by fools like me,
But only God can make a tree.

Being a poet myself, I appreciate that Kilmer writes, "Poems are made by fools like me, but only God can make a tree." This speaks to me of the impotence of man and of the omnipotence of God.

I love a 'tree view' as much as I love a 'sea view'. Both just fascinate my imagination, revealing the limitless creativity and power of God. I had to believe in that limitless power of God if I was going to survive this deadly enemy, cancer.

Perhaps my love of trees is left over from my first ancestors, Adam and Eve. Some believe this is a fantasy story for children, but today, scientists have confirmed that the human race began with one set of human parents.

Genesis 2:8-9 tells it like this, "And the Lord God planted a garden eastward in Eden and there He put the man whom He had formed out of the ground. The Lord God made to grow every TREE that is pleasant to the sight and good for food, the Tree of life also in the midst of the garden and the Tree of knowledge of good and evil."

The Genesis account goes on to tell us, "And the Lord God took the man and put him into the Garden of Eden to dress it and to keep it. And the Lord God commanded the man, saying, of every tree of the garden thou mayest freely eat. But of the tree of the knowledge of good and evil thou shalt not eat of it, for in the day that you eat thereof you shall surely die." (Gen. 2:15-17-KJV)

The rest is history. The man and his wife disobeyed God. They succumbed to the temptation of Satan to eat of the tree that God had forbidden. As God declared, in that very day, Adam and Eve died. Not physically, that would come later, but spiritually. They were separated from God, as was the whole human race from that moment on.

Death is separation from life. God is Life. However, thousands of years later, around 29-30 A.D., Jesus came on the scene, saying, "Most assuredly, I say to you, unless one is born again, he cannot see the kingdom of God." (John 3:3-NKJV)

Jesus was speaking to Nicodemus, a very religious Jew. Nicodemus asked this question, "How can a man be born when he is old? He cannot enter a second time into his mother's womb and be born, can he?" This conversation is recorded in John 3:1-7. Jesus went on to tell Nicodemus that He was speaking of a spiritual re-birth.

In the garden, man died spiritually, but Jesus says he can be born again, that is, spiritually. Not only can we be born again, but the imperative is, we MUST be born again. God gives us a second chance to renew a right relationship with Him. It was never God's intention for man to die.

Jesus says, "He who believes in Me, though he may die, he shall live. And whoever lives and believes in Me shall never die." (John 11:25-26-NKJV)

The first prophecy about Jesus (Who would be born thousands of years later) was in the Garden of Eden. Man had sinned (disobeyed God), and God said, "I will put enmity between you (Satan) and the woman, and between thy seed and her seed; it shall bruise thy head, and thou shalt bruise his heel." (Genesis 3:15)

A quote from a foot note on that portion of scripture out of the King James Study Bible says, "This verse has long been recognized as the first messianic prophecy of the Bible. Thus it also contains the first glimpse of the gospel (protoevengelium). It reveals three essential truths:

1. That Satan is the enemy of the human race, explaining why God put enmity (related to the word enemy) between thee (Satan) and the woman;
2. That He would place a spiritual barrier between thy seed (Satan's people) and
3. That the representative seed of the woman (i.e. human being; Christ) would deliver the deathblow to Satan, but in so doing would be bruised Himself. "HE" shall bruise (literally crush) thy head, but thou shall bruise his heel, refers to Christ's bruising on the cross, which led to the eventual crushing of Satan and his kingdom.

Crucifixion horribly bruises the victim's heel, as he tried desperately to push himself up in order to get air into his collapsing lungs. A bruised heel is not deadly; in contrast, a crushed head is a definite deathblow. It was at the cruel cross where Satan's plan was literally crushed to death. It is at the cross where mankind is made right with God again. The cross, of course, is made from a tree.

A tree also speaks to me of faith, life, and strength. What is the largest and oldest living thing on earth? The huge Redwood trees! We've heard the saying, "From a little acorn a mighty elm tree grows."

After my initial diagnosis of the rare aggressive cancer, Papillary Serous, and the more common cervical, I found myself immediately engaged in a struggle of faith about my own healing. Would Jesus heal me? I knew He could, but would He? Is healing just a random act of His generosity, and would I be one to be blessedly picked for this miraculous favor?

Like Job in the Bible, I had some thoughts and questions about God. As Job struggled to understand God after being stripped of his family, his health, and wealth, God asks some hard questions of Job. Job borders on blaming God for his calamities. However, in all fairness to Job, he made this proclamation in the midst of his losses, "Though He slay me, yet will I trust in Him." God demands answers from Job, which Job is unable to give. Among the many questions asked, God begins with, "Where were you when I laid the foundations of the earth? Declare if you have understanding." (Job 38:4) In other words, God asks us to trust Him without understanding Him.

The Bible says His ways are past finding out. Isaiah 55:8-11 says this, "For my thoughts are not your thoughts, neither are your ways my ways, declares the Lord. As the heavens are higher than the earth, so are my ways higher than your ways, and my thoughts than your thoughts. As the rain and the snow come down from heaven, and do not return to it without watering the earth and making it bud and flourish, so that it yields seed for the sower and bread for the eater, so is my word that goes out from my mouth: It will not return to me empty, but will accomplish what I desire and achieve the purpose for which I sent it."

One scripture that began as a mustard seed of faith in my heart and would grow into a huge TREE of faith, was a prophecy of Isaiah written some 700 years before Christ was born. This magnificent scripture is found in the Book of Isaiah, chapter 53 (I mention it often). "He was wounded for our transgressions, He was bruised for our iniquities; the chastisement of our peace was upon Him, and with His stripes we are healed." This prophecy pictures the scourging, the wounding, and the whipping that Jesus suffered at the hands of the Roman government during the week that He was tried, falsely convicted, and crucified.

I read that scripture time and time again. I slowly began to believe that the whipping Jesus took by the Romans, mysteriously and miraculously paid for my healing. My healing would not be just a random act of kindness on His part, but in God's economy, my healing was already paid for. We incredulously ask, how? God answers us, "For My thoughts are not your thoughts, nor are your ways My ways, says the LORD. For as the heavens are higher than the earth, so are My ways higher than your ways, and My thoughts than your thoughts."

My part was not to understand, but to believe and receive by faith His Word that He had sent to accomplish His purpose. In my case, He sent His word to heal me.

Often times, we are asked to have faith without understanding. What mere mortal man can understand the immortal God, Creator of the universe? Psalm 139:6 says, "Such knowledge is too high. I cannot attain unto it." We do understand that God is a holy God, and there is none like Him. As faith takes hold, so does some understanding. Faith is not blind. It is based on the Word of God, and on the reality of facts and reason.

Under the inspiration of the Holy Spirit, I wrote this song about faith, taken out of the faith chapter, Hebrews 11.

Faith

By Sande Schones

Faith is believing what you cannot see,
By faith I believe that Jesus died for me.
I wasn't there on Calvary that day,
Yet I believe what the Bible has to say.
Faith is the substance of things hoped for.
By faith I believe you can open any door.
Faith is the evidence of things not seen.
Faith is one way, there is no in between.
Through faith we understand that God spoke a word, stretched out His hand.
The things we see here, were made of things that don't appear.

Without faith, we cannot please the Lord.
We must believe He is and that He gives a good reward.
Sarah conceived and delivered a son, for she judged Him to be the Faithful One.
By faith the walls of Jerico fell down.
By faith the Red Sea opened and they walked on dry ground.
Women received their dead raised to life again.
Faith is what made Abraham God's friend.
There remains Faith Hope and Love.
All are given by the Father above.
There remains Faith Hope and Love.

So, it is by faith that we believe the record of God sending His Son Jesus to be the substitute for our sin. In the garden, after Adam and Eve partook of the forbidden fruit of the tree not necessarily an apple (the scripture does not say) their eyes were opened and they knew they were naked; they sewed fig leaves together for themselves making a covering for their nakedness. They heard the voice of the Lord God walking in the garden in the cool of the day; and Adam and his wife hid themselves from the presence of the Lord God amongst the trees of the garden, (there's those trees again), and the Lord God called unto Adam and said unto him, "Where are you?" and he said "I heard your voice in the garden and I was afraid because I was naked and hid myself". Genesis 3:21 goes on to say "Unto Adam also and to his wife did the Lord God make coats of skins and clothed them". (KJV)

This was the first shedding of blood on the earth. In order for God to make coats of skin for them, an animal had to be killed. Obviously fig leaves were not the fashion God had in mind. Imagine the Creator having to kill, with plenty of bloodshed, suffering and sorrow, one of His beloved animals. Imagine the soft trusting brown eyes of a furry non ferocious animal looking with trusted fondness into the eyes of his kind creator. God's own heart must have been broken to shed the blood of this innocent creature. That was the first blood sacrifice and the foundation of all the blood sacrifices of the Jewish religion. It was and is God's standard of covering sin. "Without the shedding of blood, there is no remission of sin". (Heb. 9:22)

Later, the Jews would sacrifice lambs, goats, or doves in honor of the first shedding of blood in the garden. This sacrifice or shedding of blood was a reminder; a covering for sin.

At the time in Egypt when the Israelites had been enslaved for 400 years and they were about to be freed, Moses heard from God to tell Pharaoh to let His people go. Pharaoh refused time after time. Each time he refused to let the people go, God struck the Egyptians with numerous and varied plagues. Finally an edict was proclaimed: The first born in all the land including Pharaoh's own household would be struck dead by a death angel. God instructed Moses; "Have each household slay a lamb and put the blood of the lamb on the door posts and when the death angel sees the blood it will pass over you". (Exodus 12:13)

To this day, Passover is celebrated by Jewish and Christian communities alike. It was and is a picture of sacrifice and deliverance of a forthcoming savior, Jesus, who would be sacrificed for us and deliver us from the bondage of sin.

When John the Baptist, Jesus' cousin, saw Jesus as a grown man, he declared: "behold the Lamb of God who takes away the sin of the world". (John 1:29)

It all fits together so perfectly. It amazes me that everyone cannot see this truth. But as the verse says in Amazing Grace: "I once was lost but now am found, was blind but now I see". If you cannot "see" this truth, ask Jesus who came to open the eyes of the blind (spiritually and physically) to open your eyes and you too will see this glorious truth.

The Apostle Paul, writing to the Corinthian Church described the last supper that Jesus ate with his disciples the night before his crucifixion, "For I received from the Lord what I also passed on to you: The Lord Jesus, on the night he was betrayed, took bread and when He had given thanks He broke it and said, "This is my body, which is for you. Do this in remembrance of me". In the same way, after supper, He took the cup saying; "This cup is the new covenant in my blood; do this whenever you drink it in remembrance of me". For whenever you eat this bread and drink this cup, you proclaim the Lord's death until He comes" (1Corinthians 11:23-26)

In taking of the cup of communion we are proclaiming his death which provides healing and also we are proclaiming that He will come again just as He promised!

Never denigrate the blood of Jesus. It is the whole world's (individually and collectively) most precious, valuable, and costly commodity. If you don't understand it, then simply "stand under" it by faith.

Jesus Himself said, "For God so loved the world, that He gave his only Son, that whosoever believes in Him should not perish but have eternal life". (John 3:16)

Eternal life is accomplished at the cross. On that TREE Jesus took all our sins upon himself and the sin of the entire world. Because He was condemned; we are pardoned. He was made to be sin for us. Jesus, the Lamb of God, who knew no sin. God is a Holy God.

The Bible says God cannot look upon sin, hence, while on the cross Jesus cries out "My God My God why have you forsaken me"? Jesus' final words on the cross: "It is finished"! He died paying the ultimate price. The Wrath of God (against sin) was satisfied. God is no longer angry at us as Jesus took our place so we could be friends with God. Believing this and receiving Him saves us for all eternity. It happened on a TREE!

Because of my love of trees, I've written several songs and poems about them. This song is about the tree on which Jesus was crucified. Strangely, it haunted me that Jesus being the creator of all things, would be tortured to death by His creation (people) and on his creation (the tree).

Lend me your imagination for a moment …

Destiny
By Sande Schones

Once upon a time a long long time ago
God made a little seed and it began to grow.
It grew and grew and it became a tree.
Let me tell you of its destiny.
For it had a purpose, just as everything.
On it one day would die a King.
Even the one who first made the tree.
That seemed to be His destiny.
So once upon a time and not so long ago,
Jesus died because He loved us so.
I don't know what became of that cross on Calvary
But I know what became of Jesus, and what becomes of me.
Because He lives now, He lives for me.
I'll live with Him forever and that's my destiny.
But could it be?
Oh could it be?
That the tree might have cried on which Jesus died that day?

Another poem I particularly love about a tree was sent to me in a card from my friends Patti Hyatt and Elaine Chamberlain. I had returned home from Providence Hospital to recuperate from the initial cancer surgery. This poem encouraged me greatly as I was faced with a battle between weakness and strength.

The Mighty Oak Tree

A mighty wind blew night and day. It stole the oak trees leaves away.
Then snapped its bough and pulled its bark
Until the oak was tired and stark.
But still the oak tree held its ground
While other trees fell all around.
The weary wind gave up and spoke
"How can you still be standing, oak"?
The oak tree said, "I know that you can break each branch of mine in two, and carry every leaf away. Shake my limbs and make me sway.
But I have roots stretched in the earth
Growing stronger since my birth.
You'll never touch them, for you see,
They are the deepest part of me.
Until today I wasn't sure
Of just how much I could endure.
But now I've found with thanks to you,
I'm stronger than I ever knew".

Like the Oak tree, the roots of my life had been growing stronger, daily, since my new birth in 1965.

Roots

"As you have therefore received Christ Jesus the Lord, so walk YE in Him: rooted and built up in Him and established in the faith, as you have been taught, abounding in it with thanksgiving"
(Col. 2:6,7) NKJV

I knew the roots of my life were planted in solid ground when I accepted Jesus as my Savior at the age of 23. Much can be said and even made fun of the term "born again", but I was truly born again at this time in my life. Jesus emphatically said: "Unless a man (or woman) is born again he cannot see the Kingdom of God". (John 3:3)

I was married and had two children, Janet and Mile. Kristin and Tanny would be added later. My high school friend, Joyce, and I had married two of Newport Harbor High Schools baseball stars; Roy Dalton and Jim Schones. We'd continued our friendship after high school and by this age we had both become bored with being housewives. You've heard of the popular television series 'Housewives of Orange County'? In the early 1960's Joyce and I were literally the original "Housewives of Orange County".

Jim was a commercial fisherman. He fished out of the ports of Newport Beach, Catalina, San Pedro and Santa Barbara. Joyce's husband, Roy, was honing his skills at becoming one of the finest cabinet makers in all of Orange County.

On occasion, when Jim was gone fishing and Roy was working late in his shop, Joyce and I would get baby sitters and visit a hot spot in Costa Mesa called Bill's Martinis. We'd have a few drinks and dance and flirt with cute guys. We thought we were pretty "hot stuff" and we were having a great time. We both knew though that we were treading on dangerously thin ice. Joyce and I had both been raised in traditional Christian homes. Joyce's dad was president of the local Bible College in Costa Mesa now known as Southern California Vanguard Liberal arts College.

My dear friend Joyce.

During high school years my sister Barbara and I, along with our parents, faithfully attended a church in Costa Mesa.

On a particular day in February ... Washington's Birthday ... I called Joyce early in the morning and said, "Hey, let's get baby sitters and go to Bill's Martinis. We can get an early start on the holiday! The high school kids are out of school today ... Lucky us"!

Joyce sounded a little pre-occupied and said, "I'll call you back. I have something to tell you".

I waited for her phone call, anticipating the fun we'd have. I imagined that she'd call me back any minute, telling me she'd changed the color of her hair. Joyce was, and still is, a very beautiful and sexy woman. She had long luxurious blonde hair. She'd switch it to red or auburn or maybe even a dark brown and perhaps even cut it into a new style whenever the whim hit her. Any changes she made only enhanced her already vivacious personality and looks.

The phone rang; it was Joyce. Before she could say what was on her mind, I blurted out … "I know, You've changed the color of your hair".

Well, she had not changed the color of her hair at all. She had changed the color of her whole life! She hesitated slightly; "Uh, Sande" she began, "I, uh … I gave my life to Jesus", she stammered into the phone.

My heart and thoughts raced as I tried to absorb the meaning of her words. The power of her statement slowly took root in my mind. I knew what she meant. She need not say another word. My heart sank to my toes. There went my fun time, get out of the boring routine, mix it up a little beautiful girlfriend. I don't really remember how that conversation ended as I was in a state of saddened shock knowing our friendship ended that very day … or so I thought.

There's a song by Michael Smith that I love. "Friends". Part of the words go like this:

"Friends are friends forever if the Lord's the Lord of them, and a friend will not say never, 'cause the welcome will not end. Though it's hard to let you go into the Father's arms, we know that a lifetime's not too long to live as friends".

I didn't know it at the time, but Joyce would be my friend for a lifetime. What I did know was that it was hard for me to let her go and she was definitely in the Father's arms.

While Joyce and I had begun spending those 'fun times' at Bill's Martinis, reality told us what we knew in our hearts; we were headed down an entangling, dark, and slippery slope. It was really only a matter of time as to who would wake up first. Somehow Joyce had heard the alarm! Miraculously she had gotten off that dark path to nowhere. She had found the Way that Jesus spoke of when He said, "Follow Me, I am the Way, I am the Truth, I am the Life". (John 14:6)

Jesus gives us insight into Truth; He says: "The thief comes to steal, kill, and destroy. I have come that you might have life and have life more abundantly". (John 10:10)

Jesus said: "Enter through the narrow gate. For wide is the gate and broad is the road that leads to destruction and many enter through it. But small is the gate and narrow the road that leads to life and only a few find it". (Matthew 7:13, 14) NIV

I am 66 as I write this. One does not need a vivid imagination to know what my life would have become had I continued on that road. My favorite drink was a 'Boiler Maker'; a shot of whiskey chased by a beer. I smoked two packs of Marlboro cigarettes a day; (and yes, I did inhale). I hate to consider a path that could have led to adultery, possibly divorce and who knows how many broken relationships? Yes! The thief comes to kill, steal, and destroy!

As Jesus relentlessly pursued me, this scripture continually plagued me in my waking hours and in my dreams: "If any man will come after me, let him deny himself and take up his cross, and follow me. For whosoever will save his life shall lose it, and whosoever will lose his life for my sake shall find it. For what is a man profited if he shall gain the whole world and lose his own soul? Or what shall a man give in exchange for his soul?" (Matthew 16:24-26) KJV

What a question to ponder!!

"The Word of God is living and powerful and sharper than any two-edged sword". (Hebrews 4:12a) NKJ

That sharp, cutting sword seemed to stab at my heart: "What are you doing? Where are you going? How is this affecting your children? What is this profiting you as a person, as a wife, as a mother? Was I actually willing to give up my eternal soul for a life of sin"?

Romans 8:20 says: "For the creation (including all of us) was subjected to futility (emptiness, fragility, and folly) not willingly (creation had no choice in this matter) but because of Him (God) who subjected it in hope". (NKJV)

In other words, I've heard it explained and illustrated like this: Man is made with a God shaped hole in his heart. That hole can be filled to satisfaction with nothing but God Himself. He made us that way in order that we might search for Him; and finding Him we find the true treasure that we all seek; LIFE. The Bible promises that we will indeed find Him if we search for Him. He has a great plan for our lives!

"For I know the thoughts that I think toward you, says the Lord. Thoughts of peace and not of evil. To give you a future and a hope. Then you will call upon Me and go and pray to Me, and I will listen to you. And you will seek me and find Me when you search for Me with all your heart". (Jeremiah 29:11-13) NKJV

We (God's creation) will never find what we search for in another person, a relationship, a drug, alcohol, food, travel, success, physical beauty, romance, money, a career, or you fill in the blanks. Our hearts are restless until we rest in God.

Within a year of that fateful phone call I too found that straight and narrow way. Joyce's continual prayers for me paid off in eternal dividends.

Once Joyce and I hungered and thirsted for good times that never seemed to satisfy; now we hungered and thirsted for the Word of God. We were blessed beyond measure! The cups of our lives were full and running over. "Blessed are those who hunger and thirst after righteousness, for they shall be filled". (Matthew 5:6)

Following is one of the first songs I wrote after being born again. I've sung it hundreds of times and I never tire of its simple melody and lyrics.

Thirsty

I was so thirsty … Thirsty was I.
I found a well, but the well ran dry.
I was so hungry … Hungry was I.
I found some bread, but it didn't satisfy.
I was always searching … searching in vain.
Searching for a rainbow after the rain.
Then I met Jesus, … Oh what a Man.
He holds my desires in the palm of His hand.
Oh what a blessing … Oh yes it's a treat.
Just to sit and learn at His feet.
Sit at his feet … Walk by His side.
Raised to the Heavens to be His bride.
He gave me Himself … and I'm no longer bored.
Who needs a rainbow when you've got the Lord!
I'm no longer thirsty … No longer thirsty am I
I found a river that will never run dry.
I'm no longer hungry … No longer hungry am I
He's the bread of Life and He does saisfy.
HE'S THE BREAD OF LIFE AND HE DOES … YES HE DOES
SATISFY!!

Another song I've written is taken from the account of the woman who met Jesus at a well. She was an immoral woman, shunned by society. Yet Jesus found her worthy to have this revealing conversation with her. You can read this amazing story in John Chapter 4:1-29. Written in the first person, I relate their conversation in this song:

Woman at the Well

I went to the well one day to draw some cool water.
There I met a man … This man called me daughter.
Well I've been called a lot of names, daughter was not one.
Could this be Messiah, for Messiah shall surely come.
"I asked what have you to do with me, for I'm a Samaritan, And
You're a man from Galilee."
He said if you only knew who I am,
You'd ask for living water, and you'd never thirst again.
"Sir I said give me a drink, so I don't have to come back here".
He said "get your husband, I've got some things I want you to hear".
"I have no husband". He said, "I know that's true,
For you've had five before, and now this man's just livin' with you".
Well, I've known a lot of men, but never a man like this one.
Could this be Messiah? For Messiah shall surely come.
I know when Christ shall come, all thing's He'll tell to me.
He looked into my eyes and He said: "I AM HE".
Well I went running into town, and I told everyone I found …
Come meet a man who told me all I've ever done.
Could this be Messiah? YES MESSIAH HAS SURELY COME".

Joyce and I got together often and prayed and read the Bible, thinking about and discussing the wonderful Word of God. Without realizing it, our roots were growing ever more deeply into the lifesaving, glorious truths of the Bible.

Oregon or Bust--1969

"Now the Lord had said to Abram, Get out of your country and from your family and from your father's house, to a land that I will show you." (Genesis 12:1) "By faith Abraham, when he was called to go out into a place which he would later receive for an inheritance, obeyed, and he went out not knowing where he was going."
(Hebrews 11:8)

Like Abraham, we were packing up, leaving all of our family and friends in California and going to a place we did not know--Newport, Oregon--to the Great Northwest. Talk about an adventure!

Jim was a native Californian, born and raised in the Golden State. I was the Kansas farm girl, transplanted to California in 1956.

Jim and I attended the same high school in Newport Beach, California, but we never met on campus. He had graduated and I was a junior in high school when I met him at a party in Balboa during 'Easter Week' (now referred to as Spring Break). Back in those days, 'Easter Week' was a wild party time--not a very wholesome time for the young people of that era. Little did I know how the true meaning of Easter would become one of the most precious and endearing meanings in my life, quite contrary to 'The Easter Week of Balboa'-- drinking, going to wild parties, and sun-burning our skin in skimpy bikinis on the beach.

We waited for the sun to go down so we could party on! Jim and I met at one of those wild parties. Jim wrote my phone number on the dash of his hot '56 Chevy. Our first date was at the Paulo Drive-in Theatre. I knew on that first date that I would marry Jim Schones.

So, in 1960, I graduated from high school, Jim and I married, and I became a mother, all in that momentous year.

In 1966, Jim was albacore fishing in a 40-foot schooner-type boat off the coast of Oregon. He unloaded fish at Peterson's fish plant in Coos Bay and ultimately found a market for crabs in Newport, Oregon.

Jim's crewmember was Denny Burke, a young kid he'd met on the docks of Newport Beach. Denny was home from Vietnam and anxious to get started at living a real life away from the sounds of war. On November 1st, 1969, a day after Janet's 9th birthday (Halloween), we loaded our furniture into Jim's '56 Chevy pick up. Six-year-old Michael climbed with Denny into his '54 Dodge flat bed. Janet and baby Kristin, six weeks old, were tucked in the back seat of my 1963 LeMans, and we headed for our new home with a huge orange pumpkin on the back of the Chevy truck and a sign that read: "Oregon or Bust!"

We loved living in Oregon. It was like being on a continuous vacation. We bought an old house on three acres in South Beach. Baby Sandra Dawn was added to our happy family in 1973.

I attended a church in Newport and joined a great organization, Fishermen's Wives. I volunteered at our local school. The kids rode motorcycles, bikes and horses. We had chickens, ducks, goats, rabbits, cats and dogs. We went berry picking, grew a big garden, cooked our crab out of doors in a big stainless steel tub, and cut our own firewood.

We participated in county fairs, baseball games, and cub scouts, took piano and dance lessons, and attended sessions of recitals and performances.

Life just kept on happening with its good, bad, and 'beautiful', until August 12th, 2008, when it all just seemed to come to a sudden, screeching halt.

I'd been experiencing a light discharge for several months, and thought it was probably due to the trauma my body had experienced going through the triple by-pass six months earlier. I decided it was time to see my gynecologist. I was shocked when the doctor looked at my records and informed me that it had been almost six years since I'd been in for a pap test. "Time goes by fast when you're having fun", so the saying goes. Actually, I didn't go to my regular checkups because, yes, time does have a way of getting away from you, but I just flat out did not like going to the doctor.

On a spiritual level, I think sometimes we don't give ourselves a spiritual checkup because we don't like taking the time. Maybe we're just too busy or having way too much fun. Perhaps we don't care for the message or, for that matter, the messenger (just a thought). Life can take hold of us instead of us taking hold of life.

Dr. Marcose was very thorough with the exam. She was seriously concerned and biopsied some suspicious cells. The examination seemed to last forever. She immediately made an appointment for an internal ultrasound. I was to return to her office the following week to discuss the test results. As I prepared to leave the examination room, I turned to her and gingerly asked,

"Do you think it could be cancer?" I was not prepared, in the slightest, for her answer.

"Yes, I do," she answered matter-of-factly. Seeing the look of unrepressed shock on my face, she quickly back-peddled, "Well, maybe not. Let's wait and see what the ultrasound reveals."

It was a long, grueling week, anticipating what could be. Jim gave me as much encouragement as he could, but we both just stumbled along, clinging to each other through the seemingly endless seven days.

Which Way to Go

"Teach me your way, O Lord, and lead me in a smooth path, because of my enemies."
(Psalm 27:11)

The agonizingly slow week finally came to an end. We found ourselves waiting anxiously in Dr. Marcos' office. She entered the room with an attending nurse, who handed her a clipboard with the anticipated file. Dr. Marcos seated herself in front of us (Jim and myself). Silently, she methodically flipped through the conclusive report.

She slowly raised her eyes to meet ours. I barely remember a word she said, except for, "I'm so sorry," as she struggled to give us more than a conciliatory smile. Any pent-up hope that I had for a good report came crashing down.

I felt a death sentence hanging over me. Her words sounded distant, muffled. She explained that she was not qualified to do this type of surgery, and suggested that we see a gynecological surgeon--a specialist--as soon as YESTERDAY! Time was of the essence!!

We stumbled from her office, partially blinded by fear and disbelief, our eyes brimming with unshed tears. We made our way to the parking lot where, somehow, we found our car. Letting the tears fall unabashedly, we began to collect our thoughts. We decided to call a family conference that night at our home in South Beach. We first called our daughter, Kristin, who lived close by the Corvallis Clinic in Independence. We didn't want to alarm her with the panic that we felt, so we told her we were calling a family conference and wanted her to come to the coast for the evening.

Several times a year, we hold a family meeting to discuss financial situations regarding our fishing vessel, The Collier Brothers.

Our boat the F/V Collier Brothers.
Our son Michael is the Captain.

Captain Mike on our boat.

Kristin is the bookkeeper, Mike skippers the boat, Janet is the manager of our South Beach property, and Tanny is the acting president of our incorporated Espress-Go business. Kristin wanted to know which of the entities we'd be discussing. I hesitated, then as nonchalantly as I could, I said, "Well actually, Kristin, we're over here at the Clinic. I've had some tests run and the Doctor just told us that I have cancer."

The silence was deafening. I continued with a tremor in my voice, but determined to sound positive. "We want the family together so we can tell everyone at once and decide what steps to take."

Kristin was incredulous. "Are you kidding?" (I wished I was.) "Where are you right now?" she asked.

"We're sitting in the parking lot at the clinic."

"I'll be right there."

"No … No … just come over tonight."

"No!" she insisted, "I'll meet you there in the parking lot in 15 minutes."

From that point on, everything was a blur. Kristin took matters into her own hands. Within 15 minutes, she'd arrived, made phone calls on her cell to Oregon Health Science University (OHSU), Providence Hospital in Portland, and the office at the Clinic to determine exactly what our choices were.

We drove to the nearest Staples, where she promptly faxed a report of Dr. Marcos' findings to the above-mentioned facilities. Before many minutes had passed, we were set to see a Dr. Paul Kucera in Portland in two short days. OHSU was over a month away, and at least we had a set date with Dr. Kucera at Providence. We could always change our minds if, after our meeting, we decided differently.

The book of Proverbs says, "There is wisdom in a multitude of councilors." That evening, returning from Dr. Marcos' stunning diagnosis, we gathered in my living room, literally dumbfounded. Here was an emotional, physical, and spiritual challenge that I never dreamed I'd have to face.

Kristin made phone calls to all her siblings to alert them, but the official word would come from Jim and me.

Our family gathering that night included our oldest daughter, Janet, and her husband, Brian; Mike, our son, and his wife, Cheryl; and Kristin, our middle daughter. Tanny was living in San Francisco and was unable to be present on such short notice. In the meantime, Kristin, Janet, and Brian looked up on the computer "Papillary Serous Cancer Stage 4", which was part of the diagnosis. We gathered in our living room that evening, shedding tears of unbelief. We prayed that God would direct us.

Being in the fishing business, Jim and I had been in stormy seas before (the most frightening for me was the Bermuda Triangle), but these were uncharted, treacherous waters. As the sun sank in the Pacific that evening, a half a mile from our home, any hope I had seemed to sink with that setting sun.

Dr. Kucera's office confirmed with us that he could see us within a week. OHSU was my personal preference, but we could not get an appointment for over a month. I say 'us' and 'we', because from that moment on, it was not just me, it was 'us'. Every hospital and doctor's visit included an entourage of from six to eight people--Jim, our kids-- Tanny flew in from San Francisco. My sister and her daughter, Robin, flew in from San Diego to sit in on consultations of surgery, therapy, timelines, and stages.

When cancer strikes, it's like a dirty bomb. It does not target one victim. It explodes into the many lives of those who are in the radius of the victim.

In the ensuing days, we called Cancer Institutes of America and found they were located in four cities in the U.S. We were more than willing to go. We kept in contact with OHSU. We contacted Loma Linda in Southern California, inquiring of a new treatment. I was very hopeful of going there, as Loma Linda is on the cutting edge of new cancer research, but disappointment loomed like a dark cloud when they confirmed that I was not a candidate for that particular treatment.

We contemplated Mexico, Canada, and New York. My Chiropractor nephews in California and Oregon sent prayers and ideas on supplements and healthy diets. We contacted a naturopathic doctor in Portland who had been recommended to us. Which way? Which way to go? Would God just show us what to do? Where to go?

When Mike was a young boy, he belonged to Cub Scouts. I was his den mother. Our group learned a song and performed it at one of the meetings.

"Which way, America? Which way to go?
    I love my country land; I want to know,
    Which way America is going to go?
    There's plenty of roads to travel; there's plenty of roads to take
    I'm gonna ask the Lord above, which is the road to take."

Like the song, we had many a roads to travel, many a roads to take; and like the song, we solemnly asked the Lord, which road to take.

Since becoming that young Christian girl, back in 1965, my first line of defense has been, and always will be, the Word of God.

We read Isaiah 42:16, "I will bring the blind by a way they did not know. I will lead them in ways they have not known. I will make darkness light for them and crooked places straight. These things I will do for them and not forsake them." Those were powerful words to us, laced with hope. He would be with us and show us what to do--where to go!

Somewhere in the twilight of this burgeoning nightmare, these words came to me, "The Lord is my light and my salvation, whom shall I fear? The Lord is the strength of my life; of whom shall I be afraid?"

I knew it was in the Bible, but I didn't know exactly where. Looking it up in a concordance, I found it to be Psalm 27. At the time, I didn't realize what an integral, powerful part Psalm 27 would play in my life. From that Psalm, I indulged my spiritual senses in hundreds and hundreds of words from the Psalms. I highly encourage the reading of the Psalms on a daily basis, whether you're in the thick of the battle or in the thick of peace.

After finding the location of Psalm 27 and reading it in its entirety, I found those powerful words directly speaking to me of my situation.

The Word of God is like that. It is not ancient. It is not modern. It is ETERNAL, and it is relevant, instantly, in any day of any generation, past, present, or future. Here is Psalm 27, written by King David some three thousand years ago. In parenthesis are my personal thoughts.

"The Lord is my light and my salvation; Whom shall I fear?
The Lord is the strength of my life; Of whom shall I be afraid?
(*Shall I be afraid of cancer? Quite honestly, I was terrified.*)
When the wicked came against me to eat up my flesh (*cancer*),
My enemies and foes (*cancer*), they stumbled and fell.
(*Wow! This is past tense; this is Faith!*)
Though an army may encamp against me,
(*Cancer was a dreaded army that had set up camp against me.*)
My heart shall not fear; Though war may rise against me,
(*This was war; later one of Dr. Kucera's nurses said to my children; "She'll be in for the fight of her life."*)
In this will I be confident.
One thing I have desired of the Lord, That will I seek:
That I may dwell in the house of the Lord, all the days of my life,
And to behold the beauty of the Lord, and to inquire in His temple.
For in the time of trouble,
(*And I was surely in big trouble.*)
He shall hide me in His pavilion;
In the secret place of His tabernacle He shall hide me;
He shall set me high upon a rock.
And now my head shall be lifted up above my enemies all around me;
Therefore I will offer sacrifices of joy in His tabernacle;
I will sing, yes, I will sing praises to the Lord.
(*My friend, Chris Watkins, literally prophesied to me that I would live, for I had more songs to write and sing for the Lord.*)

Hear, O Lord, when I cry with my voice.
Have mercy also upon me and answer me.
When you said, "Seek My face," My heart said to You,
"Your face, Lord, I will seek."
Do not hide your face from me;
Do not turn your servant away in anger.
You have been my help;
Do not leave me nor forsake me, O God of my salvation.
When my father and my mother forsake me,
Then the Lord will take care of me.
Teach me YOUR WAY
(*Which way should we go, Lord?*)
And lead me in a smooth path, because of my enemies.
Do not deliver me to the will of my adversaries;
(*I knew that cancer's will was to kill me.*)
For false witnesses have risen against me, and such as breathe
out violence.
(*Cancer is one of the most violent of all diseases.*)
I would have lost heart, unless I had believed that I would see the
goodness of the Lord in the LAND OF THE LIVING.
(*I began to believe that I would be found at the end of this pilgrimage
in the Land of the Living.*)
Wait on the Lord;
Be of good courage, and He shall strengthen your heart;
Wait, I say, on the Lord."
(*I knew this was not going to be an overnight stay, and I would have to
trust and wait on the Lord.*)

In the column of my Bible, I wrote, "This is my banner Psalm for this
trial of my life and faith--8/24/08." I probably read this Psalm every
night for months and months, along with many of the other Psalms,
which brought such peace and faith to my heart. The reference,
Psalm 27, ended up on at least 80 T-shirts around Newport. More
about that later.

But for now, I'd have to wait on the Lord for His direction of which way to go. "For we have no power to face this vast army that is attacking us. We do not know what to do, but our eyes are on you." (II Chronicles 20:12)

As we waited on the Lord, we stood on this promise, "In all your ways acknowledge Him, and He will direct your paths." (Proverbs 3:6)

Team Sande

"Know you not, that they which run in a race run all, but one receives the prize? So run, that you may obtain."
(I Corinthians 9:24)

Team Sande getting ready for battle on operation day.

In the sport of racing, as in any competitive sport, when the athlete wins, it is a win for their school, college, or for their entire nation, as in the Olympics.

We are a baseball and softball family. As I said earlier, I married Jim, Newport Harbor High Schools baseball star. My dad, Maxie, played first base for the American Legion team after World War II. On a warm summer night in 1948 in Osborne, Kansas, he was tragically killed. I was just five years old. His team was scheduled to play the next day, Sunday. In the sudden tragedy of his untimely death, his team decided to play in his honor, not cancelling the game. They won.

My first encounter with baseball was at that country school in Kansas. Remember? The one with the mean teachers. They were gentler and kinder out on the baseball field at noon hour and recesses.

Our three girls, Janet, Kristin, and Tanny, all played college softball. I've always been proud of that. I can still see Mike, age 9, on Betty Wheelers' Field on third base, straining for an incoming ball thrown by an outfielder teammate.

Janet's three daughters, Ashley, Savanah, and Riley, all played little league, Jr. Varsity, and Varsity softball through their high school years. Ashley played her first year in college. Mike and Cheryl's girls, Madison and Megan, played Varsity softball for Newport High School. Our grandson, Beaux, played Little League and High School baseball. Ashley and Savanah played on the Newport High School championship team in 2002. They had been trained as 9-12 year olds from 1995-1997, under the excellent coaching of Richard Beloni and Brian Berg, and as they moved into high school years, under Coach Spencer.

As a side bar, let me say, in a very real way, this reflects training our young people to be champions in this game we play called life.

When we gathered for prayer, as a family, that first night, the idea was brought up that we would face this giant, cancer, as a team. Statistics said we were outnumbered; it looked like cancer was favored to win.

When a popular drive-thru coffee company (Dutch Brothers) set up business just a mile from our drive-thru coffee shop, I wanted to 'throw in the towel'. I didn't think I could compete. When Jim learned of my 'give up' attitude he chided, "Since when is David afraid of Goliath?" That gave me the courage to stay in the game (the coffee game). Six years later, Espressgo is still a thriving business.

But now, I would not be facing Goliath, or Dutch Brothers. I'd be facing a much more formidable foe, the 'Giant', Cancer.

An extended family member is a cancer researcher. After studying all the diagnosis information, my family asked his opinion. He sadly conceded, "I don't think she can survive this. If she were my wife or mother, I would not put her through chemo and radiation. I would let her die without the ravages of a treatment that I don't think will sustain or prolong her life in any way." When I learned of this, I literally hung my head in defeat; but my family encouraged me.

"We can win this!"

Jim's words came back to me. "Since when is David afraid of Goliath?" Quite honestly, David might not have been afraid of Goliath, but I was terrified of cancer. If David wasn't afraid of Goliath, I know that he was afraid at other times in his life, facing danger, for he wrote, "What time I am afraid, I will trust in God." (Psalm 56:3)

I tried to muster up the strength to, somehow, believe that perhaps I Could … might … maybe … possibly … hopefully beat the opponent I was facing. Again, my thoughts turned to Psalm 27. "The Lord is my light and my salvation; whom shall I fear? The Lord is the strength of my life; of whom shall I be afraid?"

Soon, the disparaging news spread in our small town of Newport; Sande Schones has been diagnosed with incurable, inoperable cancer and given little hope of survival.

Our sign at Espressgo, under Janet's mandate, would put announcements on the reader board—"Pray for Sande." "Plan for Peace: Prepare for War." "Go Team Sande." And were in it to win it!

Friends and customers would drive through for a cup of coffee and an update.

Like the song says, "I love livin' in a small town." It's true! I do!

My wonderful friend, neighbor, fellow team member, and daughter, Janet, was on the phone to her daughter, Ashley, attending college in Santa Cruz, apprising her of my situation. In their conversation, Janet said, "I've got this feeling in the pit of my stomach, like you feel when you're getting ready to play an important game with a team that's going to be hard to beat." Ashley agreed and said, "Yeah; Mom, we need some team shirts for Grandma Sande."

They decided that the original team members would be the whole family. Jesus would be the coach. I guess I would be the designated hitter. Against all odds, maybe I'd hit a homerun. We decided, together, that we would face this with all the courage and fortitude that we could muster against a team that loomed, unbeatable.

We prayed, and even laughed, and also cried. In the movie, "League of Their Own", when one of the baseball girls started crying, their coach, played by Tom Hanks, with sneering encouragement, snarled, "Crying? There's no crying in baseball." So, we dried our tears, and prayed, and believed, and hoped against hope that Jesus would coach us to victory, and that God would heal me of cancer.

The week wore on. I was scheduled for surgery in a few short days, which, by the way, turned out unsuccessful (more about that later). A day before the surgery, Kristin got a dozen royal blue T-shirts printed up with big white letters, "TEAM SANDE", and in smaller letters, "Psalm 27".

On the actual day of my surgery, August 27th, 2008, I received this note from my daughter, Kristin. She was one of the "Team Captains."

"Mom, as I put on my Team Sande shirt this morning, I felt excited. Excited for the game ahead of us. I know that we are up against a big team, but I know that it is a team that WE will defeat. God put you on this earth for a purpose and a reason. God gave us, your family, to you

41

for a purpose and a reason. You are not in this battle alone. WE are here for you and with you every step along the way. I like what Tom Baker told you about faith. (Tom is a pastor friend of our family.) "You have honored God and have raised up children of faith. And I believe that God has blessed you because of that, and I believe that God will continue to bless you." (Kristin continued) We are your faith team. When you have doubts and fears, know that we are here to lift you up every day. Also know that God is with you and all of us every step of the way. I just want you to know that I love you, and I love our family that you and Dad have given us. We are a great TEAM, and together we can face anything. Love, Sissy." (her nick name)

Soon, my granddaughters, Riley, Madison, and Megan, and their cousin, Hailey Woodard, who were softball players at Newport High School, wore their Team Sande T-shirts to school. When students in Karina Hargett's high school class began asking, "What is Team Sande, and what is Psalm 27?" she took the leap of courage to tell her class about my battle with cancer; that I'd chosen Psalm 27 from the Bible as my cheer leading song. In fact, after spending a troubled night in prayer, Mrs. Hargett took the Bible to her class the next day, and read all 14 verses of Psalm 27 to her class. When one student suggested, accusingly, that she was preaching religion to them, she emphatically replied, "The students asked, so I'm just responding to their questions."

Many of the students began ordering and wearing their Team Sande T- shirts to school. As the school year ended, I was asked to speak to Mrs. Hargett's class. I was doubly honored when Jesse Ligget, graduating senior, asked me to speak at their Baccalaureate service. Many of the students had been inspired to believe that you can achieve the impossible, or at least give it your best shot to win.

I teased Karina, later, suggesting she might end up in a courtroom, with the ACLU (American Civil Liberties Union), having to defend herself with the help of ACLJ (American Center for Law and Justice), who with bravery and victory take on many such actual cases.

As a result of the "Team Sande" T-shirts, about 80 adults and young people in our area began wearing the shirts, and praying and believing for my healing. I'd tell anyone wanting a T-shirt that they could not be a team member unless they truly believed that God would heal me.

I was unspeakably honored when Shelly Moor's H.S. Varsity Volleyball Team warmed up in their Team Sande shirts for their play-off game at the end of their 2008 season. They won! I sat in the bleachers cheering them on in my Cubs T-shirt. Yes! I like livin' in a small town. I love bragging about this great community that I became a part of back in 1969.

One day, I was listening to a popular talk show host on the radio. The conversation was on how the media can spin the truth and twist facts. They can assassinate the character of just about anyone they disagree with. In this case, it was the talk show host. When asked by his guest, "How do you survive?" the host thought for a long moment, then answered musingly, "It depends on how many people you have in the waiting room."

I've pondered a lot about that very thought provoking answer. I determined that not just on the day of my operation, or of the many treatments of radiation, internal radiation, and chemotherapy, I not only had my family and closest friends in 'my waiting room', but I had my whole community here, near, and far in my waiting room. They were rooting for me, encouraging me, believing for me, and supporting me with prayer and faith and love. I am greatly and gratefully humbled. I love living in a small town.

Go Team! ... Go! ... Fight! ... WIN!

Dr. Paul Kucera

"Those who are well have no need of a physician, but those who are sick."
(Matthew 9:12)

On a spiritual level (as that young, Orange County housewife back in 1965), I knew I was in need of a Savior--the Great Physician. I was sick with sin. Now I found myself sick with cancer and I was not in denial! I needed a physician--now! I mentioned previously that Dr. Marcos immediately confessed that she was not equipped to do the radical hysterectomy required to save my life. Time was of the essence!

We were elated to get an appointment with a Dr. Paul Kucera at Providence Hospital in Portland, Oregon, within a week's time. We were not so elated when we met Dr. Kucera in person. At that first appointment, our disappointment was palpable. Not only did Dr. Kucera seem to be elderly (in reality he was only 49 years old), but it seemed he had suffered from some kind of stroke. Talk about a 'stroke' of bad luck!!!

We had a hard time understanding him. He slurred his speech, talking out of one side of his mouth, wiping saliva as he spoke. If I described Dr. Kucera as a cartoon character, I'd say he resembled Walt Disney's 'Goofy.' He had big ears, big feet that were stuck inside huge, floppy, round-toed black shoes (probably size 16), and a very dry sense of humor. After consulting with him about the stage of cancer, procedures, time-lines, surgery, and REALITIES, he set the surgery date for just a short week away.

The procedure would be a radical hysterectomy. The time would be early morning. The date--August 26th. The expectation would be to remove the female organs in hopes of removing all cancer. However, the bitter REALITY screamed Stage 4 cancer! This was surreal. I didn't even feel sick, let alone the very real possibility--NO!--the PROBABILITY that I was dying of cancer! We were 'freaked out' at the daunting challenge that lay before us; shocked beyond belief at this turn of events in our lives. Numbly, we sat in his office trying to absorb all of the details. We intensely watched his hands to see if they shook. Our thoughts converged, "Can he possibly accomplish this delicate operation?" I cannot adequately describe my total disappointment and fear in the fact that he would be my surgeon.

Upon leaving his office, we timidly asked his nurse, Cynthia,

"Has Dr. Kucera had a stroke?"

"Oh, no," she quickly responded, "He is a 'cancer survivor' and is currently taking radiation treatments."

We breathed a sigh of relief and found some humor in the fact that we'd all noticed that his hands were very steady and sure as he wrote instructions for us to follow pre-surgery. However, I left his office that day with my head down and my feet dragging. I overheard his nurse say to my children,

"Your mother will be in for the fight of her life."

My heart sank along with any hope I had of beating this giant. I've never considered myself a fighter. As I awaited surgery day, those words repeated themselves in my mind over and over!

"Your mother will be in for the fight of her life."

I mentioned earlier that we owned a drive-thru coffee business. I suddenly recalled a conversation Jim had with me several years earlier, when Dutch Brothers Coffee came to town--a huge competition for my small espresso shop.

"What? Give up? Give in without even trying? Since when is

David afraid of Goliath?" Jim challenged me with those words. Then and Now!

The book of Ecclesiastes, written by wise King Solomon, says that, "Two are better than one because they have a good reward for their labor. For if they fall, one will pick up his companion." (Ecclesiastes. 4:9&10-NKJV) I was falling and Jim was faithful to fulfill God's word by continually picking me up.

During that long week before surgery, a friend of mine from southern California called to tell me of a friend of hers who was undergoing cancer treatment. Her friend had been transferred to Albany, Oregon. This woman's gynecologist had suggested, strongly, that if at all possible, she should get in to see the very best--a Dr. Paul Kucera who'd worked at OHSU and was now in private practice at Providence Hospital in Portland. Wow! Did that ever give us confirmation and encouragement!

The Lord speaks to us in many ways. He always speaks through His Word, but since Dr. Kucera's name is not in the Bible (I'm being silly), I believed this was a direct encouragement from God, telling me that I was in good hands with Him (JESUS) and with Dr. Kucera.

We came to love and highly respect Dr. Kucera (AKA Goofy). As surgery day approached, we determined he was anything but goofy. He was highly recommended as a surgeon, serious, conservative and forthright, with a very dry sense of humor, but a sense of humor, no less, and we desperately needed something to smile about.

Surgery Day -- August 26th

"This is the day that the Lord has made. I will rejoice and be glad in it."

We have a special devotional that we resort to on a daily basis, written by Chuck Smith, Senior Pastor of Calvary Chapel, Costa Mesa. It's a blue book entitled "Wisdom for Today". I simply refer to it as the "Blue Book". Interestingly, the automobile Blue Book records the true value of vehicles, while Pastor Chuck's Blue Book records the everyday value of God's Word.

I am often amazed at how timely the day's message is. For instance, on August 25 (pre-op day), the title of that day's message was, "The God Who Sees and Hears." At the end of the one-page daily devotion was this proclamation, "How blessed we are to serve the true and living God, the Creator of the heavens and the earth. The God Who sees, the God Who hears, and the God Who helps in time of need."

That day's devotional comforted me. I took courage being reminded that God was seeing me, hearing me, and helping me in this desperate time of need. One of the Hebrew names for God is El-Roi, "The God Who Sees."

On August 26th, the day's devotional was entitled "Step by Step." I quote several excerpts from this short, but powerful, and timely message.

"God wants us to walk by faith, so He doesn't explain His entire plan to us at once. God leads us step by step, one move of obedience and trust upon another. We don't have to have the whole picture at once. We just have to take the steps He asks us to take. Trust Him. It will be clear later."

The prayer at the end of the devotion says, "Father, help us to follow You and trust what You are doing in our lives. In Jesus' name, Amen."

This was the Big Day. This was the day that, hopefully, Dr. Kucera would perform a surgical miracle. He is one of only twelve surgeons in the state of Oregon with this particular expertise. The nurses hooked me up to IVs and gave me injections to relax me before putting me to sleep. My original "Team Sande" members hugged me, kissed me, and prayed with me as I was wheeled into the operating room. Dr. Kucera informed "The Team" that it would be a 4 or 5-hour operation. He would buzz them in the waiting room and confer with them as soon as the operation was complete.

You can imagine their hopes and fears when just a short hour and a half later, they were summoned to the waiting room to meet with Dr. Kucera. Was it a miracle? When they opened me up, was there no cancer anywhere to be found?

No! On the contrary, the lymph nodes were fully loaded with cancer, and too close to the main aorta to be removed without risk of bleeding to death. Dr. Kucera was as disappointed as they were. The cancer was 'inoperable'!

I would be sent home to recover and immediately begin chemotherapy treatments with my oncologist, Dr. Peter Kenyon. Radiation treatments would begin in Corvallis with Dr. Frye, the radiologist. Dr. Kucera's hope was to reduce the cancer in the lymph nodes in order to re-operate, giving me a chance to live.

However, we've all heard and have determined what 'inoperable' really means. I knew I was being sent home to die.

Upon my release from Providence Hospital, my immediate daily routine was Jim driving me to and from Corvallis five days a week for topical radiation treatments. Jim was a great limousine driver! On each Friday, after the three-hour round trip, I would return to Newport to undergo a three-hour infusion of chemotherapy. On the weekends, I would lie on the couch sleeping, barely able to initiate an appetite to recuperate strength to begin the stressful routine again each Monday morning.

By November, both my radiologist and my oncologist suggested that the lymph nodes were responding very positively to the treatments. Both specialists suggested that perhaps Dr. Kucera would agree and reschedule the delayed hysterectomy.

To my dismay, Dr. 'Goofy', i.e. 'Conservative', said, "NO!" In his opinion, the lymph nodes hadn't shrunk enough. He was calling the shots. Dr. Kucera was the quarterback!

I was disappointed! I had to trust that God was the director behind the scenes orchestrating this whole operation. He was the true quarterback!

At one point during a routine internal examination with Dr. Kucera, I struck up an interesting conversation with him. With my legs in the stirrups during the poking and prodding, I casually said,

"I believe in miracles." My faith must've been in high gear that day.

He responded with, "I believe in miracles, too. I believe in the miracles of chemotherapy and radiation."

We both were silent for a moment and I ventured on.

"I believe in the Great Physician and the lesser physician."

He hesitated, and then asked, "Who is the Great Physician?"

I answered, "That would be Jesus."

"And the lesser physician?" he tentatively asked. My heart was smiling inside my chest.

"That would be you," I answered.

"Well, how did Jesus heal people?" he asked. "He didn't operate on them."

"Ahh, a true surgeon," I thought.

"No, he didn't have to operate. He usually laid His hands on them and they were healed."

"For instance?" he challenged.

Interestingly, I immediately recalled the story of a woman with an issue of blood, recorded in the gospels. In my own words, I related the Biblical account to him.

"Well, a woman with an issue of blood had suffered at the hands of physicians for twelve years. When she saw Jesus passing by, she thought to herself, "If only I could but touch the hem of His garment I will be healed."

"She touched Him," I told Dr. Kucera. I continued, "Jesus immediately stopped and asked, "Who touched me?" His disciples asked Him, "What do you mean who touched you? All these people are thronging you! They're all touching you." "No!" Jesus said, "Someone has touched me in faith, for I feel that virtue has left my body."

With that, Dr. Kucera cut me off. Remember, he's ultra-conservative and all this faith talk might be a little too far out for his scientific mind. He finished the exam and dryly commented,

"We doctors only believe in miracles when there is no hope, and in your situation that is not the case."

Knowing that he was blunt, dry, and conservatively truthful, I drew in a silent gasp. Was he telling me that my case was not hopeless? This was one of the rare moments when I felt like there truly was hope for me, not only by the hand of God, but by the hand of science, as well. (However, I believe God is the Author of TRUE science.) I dared to hope, with his words ringing in my ears. Later, I found out that Dr. Kucera really didn't have much hope for me at all, and I lovingly said of him, "Doctor Kucera is a liar."

I admired several things about Dr. Kucera. He was a Fellow amongst his peers and highly respected in the medical community, and he was at the top of his field; yet he was not too proud to allow me to engage him in a conversation of faith, even to the point of him asking me sincere questions, like "How did Jesus heal people?" and "Who is the Great Physician?"

I dressed and entered his office for further consultation on my progress. Sitting in his office, with 'my team', I hoped that the exam would prove to be positive for the surgery. We waited with bated breath, anticipating Dr. Kucera's affirmation. He spoke dryly, wiping saliva from the side of his mouth.

"I am recommending more radiation."

"No!" I heard myself nearly shouting.

"No!" I repeated with absolute authority. "I will not take anymore radiation."

I meant it! I'd had enough! My skin was horribly burned from my navel to my pelvis. I had no appetite and I had constant, extreme diarrhea; I couldn't get five minutes away from a bathroom. To top it all off, the lymph nodes had not shrunk enough to operate.

"Well, this is a different kind of radiation," Dr. Kucera encouraged me. "I promise it will not mess with your appetite or your digestive system, and it will not burn you. It is done internally. It will specifically target the cervix." He sounded enthusiastic and hopeful.

Could it be my chance? Trusting him, and Him (the lesser and the Greater Physician), I conceded to go for it.

This type of radiation was only done in three areas in Oregon: Portland, Salem, and Eugene. Again, we found ourselves asking the Lord which way to go, remembering His Word, "In all your ways acknowledge Him and He shall direct your paths." (Proverbs 3:6)

Dr. Gimmel

The writer of Hebrews exhorted the Christians to be hospitable to strangers, "for by so doing some have unwittingly entertained angels." The Old Testament records numerous times when angels appeared as normal men.

We chose to have the internal radiation treatments in Eugene. In so choosing, I met 'my angel doctor', Dr. Gimmel. Salem was closer to our home. Our daughter, Tanny, now lived in Portland, having transferred from her job in San Francisco in order to be closer to us during this trying time. It would be reasonable to do the treatments in Portland in case we needed to spend the night. However, our prayers led us to Eugene.

On our first visit to the Cancer Institute, we were ushered into a tidy, compact office, where we were being instructed to register for my future appointments. There would be a series of treatments three times a week for five or six weeks.

We (Jim, Kristin, and myself) were seated at a counter with a lovely young woman on the other side who was handing us forms and pens. While Jim was filling out the forms, I noticed what appeared to be a business card holder. I reached out to take a card, thinking it would have the phone number and information of the Institute. But much to my amazement, it was a scripture card that read, "The Lord is my light and my salvation." (Psalm 27)

I was thrilled! That was the scripture the Lord had given me in the first days of this horrible battle with cancer. My 'Banner Psalm'. I handed the card to Jim and Kristin. Both their faces brightened with knowing smiles. It confirmed that we had chosen the right place. I'm sure the other two choices would've been fine, but I think God was showing us that He was with us, hearing and answering our prayers.

That little card gave us some much-needed confidence. It was as if God was touching us personally with His affirmation and love.

Finally, we were ushered into Dr. Gimmel's examining room for our first interview with her. She was like a breath of fresh air as she swirled into the room in a flurry of white, wearing her physician's lab coat. Her demeanor was that of a busy, and very much in demand, doctor. She was professional, yet very personal. She seemed uniquely attuned to me. She gave me a feeling of confidence. I don't think she weighed much over a hundred and ten pounds. Small but Mighty! She appeared to be around 30 years old with a creamy complexion and light colored hair.

A small, silver cross necklace hung about my neck. I noticed her looking at it. She surprised me by asking,

"Are you a Christian?"

I was taken aback! I didn't think physicians crossed that 'religious line', but she seemed quite sincere and genuinely interested.

"Yes, I am," I answered, anticipating her reason for asking.

"So am I," she enthusiastically responded, "and I believe, with God's help and this treatment, you will be made well." She reached out to touch me. I understood that she believed, without a doubt, that what she was predicting would certainly come to pass.

Hope literally soared into my whole being. It was like being in the company of an angel. From that time on, I referred to Dr. Gimmell as 'my angel doctor'. I told her of my Banner Psalm--Psalm 27--and how we'd prayed about where we should go for this treatment. I showed her the scripture card from the front desk. She smiled knowingly.

This was November. I would have my first treatment with her the following week. That interim week would become one of the most profound weeks of my life.

Thanksgiving, my favorite holiday, was fast approaching.

The Thanksgiving Trail

"In all things give thanks for this is the will of God in Christ Jesus for you" (I Thess. 5:18)

Between our house and Janet's (our oldest daughter), there is a marked trail, marked by trodden down grass, caused by innumerable trips from her house to mine (and vice versa). When we first moved to Oregon, we bought that little house on three acres. In time, we tore down the original house and moved our site to the back of the property. We sold the front of the property to Janet and her husband, Brian.

What a neighbor to have! I love all our neighbors, but I've got to say my favorite neighbor is Janet. Having her right next door is certainly a plus! I can't describe properly or convey my deepest appreciation for her as a friend, neighbor, and daughter.

On a minor note, one great plus is her pantry and ours. If I am lacking sugar, bread, pickles, Campbell's Soup ... WHATEVER! I just have to walk a few yards across the lawn, saving me a ten-mile round trip to the nearest grocery store.

Sometimes, though, I'll be looking in my pantry and I can't seem to find what I'm looking for. Hmmm ... could it be at my favorite neighbor's kitchen? With a smile in my heart, I'm happy to have the sweet exchange.

We usually have Thanksgiving at our house. On this Thanksgiving, 2008, our whole family was particularly thankful.

The cancer serpent, with its venomous fangs, was still threatening my life, but by God's grace, I was still alive. I was taking a product called Reliv that helped me withstand the ravages of chemotherapy and radiation. Unlike many other products that I'd tried, this one did NOT have false claims. Yes! We had a lot to be thankful for this Thanksgiving.

Our Thanksgiving tradition seats the adults at the dining room table. The grandkids find their way around various coffee and card tables set close by. Before we eat, each person says something for which they're thankful. Needless to say, the lion's share of our thanks went to God. I was still alive and able to celebrate this favorite of holidays with my family. When it was Janet's turn she simply said, "I'm thankful for the trail between my house and mom's,"—hence, "the Thanksgiving Trail". Now, every time I walk over to Janet's house (usually at least once a day), I really ponder that trail. Even when the grass is freshly cut, the trail is obviously there.

In 1960 when Janet was born, I was just a few weeks away from being all of 18 years old. Thankfully, abortion was not available. If it had been, who knows what a foolish, self-centered, immature teenager would choose. After all, I wanted to go to college. I had dreams of becoming a secretary in a prestigious corporation. I could be an airline stewardess, meeting people from all over the world. Maybe I would go to Nashville and write and sing country songs! I thank God my weak, sinful nature was not put to the test. Sometimes I think of that as I traverse the Thanksgiving Trail. What if …?

The trail also speaks to me of God's path for our lives. Jeremiah 29:11 says this, "For I know the thoughts that I think toward you, says the Lord, thoughts of peace and not of evil, to give you a future and a hope."

The Thanksgiving Trail is narrow, the width of two shoe steps, reminding me that Jesus spoke of a narrow trail that leads to life. He said, "Wide is the gate and broad is the way that leads to destruction (NKJV). Strait is the gate and narrow is the way that leads to life." (Matthew 7:14-KJV)

We often mistake the word "strait" for the word "straight". "Strait" is the Greek word, "agonizo", which means to strain. Jesus is saying we must strain to enter into the gate that leads to life. Perhaps the straining to enter in is simply straining out all the lies that mislead us. A huge lie that we tend to believe is, "We all have our own beliefs; there are many ways to God." In contrast, Jesus said, "I am The Way, The Truth, and The Life. No one comes to the Father except through me." (John 14:6) We are deceived into believing that, "I'm good enough to get into heaven. I don't steal or kill, so 'I'm good enough'." The Bible says that there is none good. No Not One. I call it 'the human condition'.

Enter GRACE--acronym: "God's Riches At Christ's Expense". Jesus paid the price, on the cross, for all our sins. Simply believing in Him and receiving Him is the door to heaven. The ultimate goal of humanity is to, one day, find our way to heaven.

Heaven is God's blessing to us, His creation.

Here is another Poem/song I wrote in 2003.

His Way
By Sande, 2003

I must go His way and not my own,
If I go His way, I'll find my way home.
For I'm just a child, sometimes lost, needing to be found
Though I've been on the road and I am homeward bound.
Sometimes I fall, sometimes I lose my way
I hear Jesus … I hear Him say,
"Follow Me, child, I am the Way."
Oh, I'm just a child, sometimes lost and undone,
To find my way home I must follow the Son.
His way's the right way and not my own
If I go His way, I'll find my way home.
I'll find my way home.

I am so very thankful to God that He opened my ears, my eyes, and my heart to follow Him on that narrow trail so many years ago. The Bible says, "In all things, give thanks, for this is God's will for you." The Bible does not instruct us to give thanks FOR all things, but IN all things. In other words, in ALL situations. I do not give thanks that I have cancer, but I give thanks to God in spite of the cancer. God is worthy of our giving of thanks, no matter what the situation. We may not understand, but He promises us in His word that, as we trust Him with our sacrifice of Thanksgiving, He, in turn, will deliver us.

There is a song that we sing in church, Blessed be Your Name, by Matt Redman

Blessed be your name, in the land that is plentiful, Where Your streams of abundance flow. Blessed be Your name.

Blessed be your name, when I'm found in the desert place, Though I walk through the wilderness, Blessed Be Your Name.

Every blessing you pour out I'll turn back to praise. When the darkness closes in, Lord still I will say …

Blessed be the Name of the Lord,
Blessed be your glorious name.
Blessed be your name when the sun's shining down on me, when
the world's all as it should be, Blessed be your name.
Blessed be your name on the road marked with suffering, though
there's pain in the offering.
Blessed be your name.
You give and take away
You give and take away
My heart will choose to say
Blessed Be Your Name.

The Bible records the situation of a child, who convulsed, foaming
at the mouth and falling on the ground. Jesus asked the father, "How
long has he been like this"? The father answered, "Since childhood.
But if you can do anything, take pity on us and help us". "If I can?"
said Jesus. "Everything is possible to him who believes". Immediately
the boy's father exclaimed "I do believe" and in the same breath he
added "Help me overcome my unbelief". The disciple Mark, who
records this event, went on to say that Jesus healed the boy.

I'm sure there were plenty of shouts of Thanksgiving as they
walked the trail toward their home.

And as we walk the trail toward our heavenly home, I pray there will
always be many shouts of Thanksgiving and praise to our wonderful
Savior and God who says: "Follow me, I am the Way".

The Smoky Bible,
My Jordan River

"He was a mighty man of valor but he was a leper"
(II Kings 5:1a)

In the book of II Kings, chapter 5, verses 1 through 14, the Bible records the story of a man by the name of Naaman. In my own words I recount the story.

Naaman was a mighty man of valor. He was captain of the host of the King of Syria. The account says he was a great man and honorable. BUT HE HAD LEPROSY. Leprosy was and still is an incurable disease. In today's world, speaking socially and physically, it could be compared to the first days and years when AIDS attracted the attention of the world.

In Israel, people with leprosy were separated from the main population, quarantined from family, friends, and community. If they were in society they would have to herald themselves, "Unclean! unclean!" in order that the main population could scatter quickly from them. Leprosy was highly contagious and carried a loathsome and demoralizing stigma.

Naaman was not an Israelite but nonetheless he, along with any other citizen of that day who had leprosy, carried this horrible burden of separation and alienation. Perhaps he had just the beginning stages, for it seems he was still carrying out his duties for the King.

In my own words the Bible account continues. A young Israelite girl had been taken captive by the Syrian army and had become a servant/slave girl to Naaman's wife. She mentioned to her master's wife that if Naaman could meet up with Elisha, a prophet from Samaria, he would recover from this dreaded disease.

When the King heard of this, he quickly sent Naaman to Israel to be healed of leprosy.

Verses 9 through 11 quotes, "Then Naaman went with his horses and chariot (I'd say with not a small amount of pomp and circumstance), and he stood at the door of Elisha's house and Elisha sent a messenger unto him, saying, 'Go and wash in the Jordan seven times and your flesh shall be restored to you and you shall be clean.' But Naaman became furious and went away and said, 'Indeed, I said to myself, He will surely come out to see me and stand and call on the name of the Lord his God and wave his hand over the place and heal the leprosy. Are not the Abanah and the Pharpar, the rivers of Damascus, better than all the waters of Israel? Could I not wash in them and be clean?' So he turned and went away in a rage." (NKJV)

It didn't exactly happen the way Naaman had envisioned. The great prophet of Israel, Elisha, did not come out personally to heal the great Captain, Naaman. Instead, Elisha sent a mere messenger to Naaman, telling him to go wash in the Jordan seven times and he would be healed of leprosy.

Naaman was furious! He was a great man, well deserving of respect! His importance should surely have prompted Elisha's personal attention. That deceitful destroyer, FALSE PRIDE, had reared its ugly head.

This account of Naaman had such significance that Jesus referenced it some 700 years later. (Luke 4:27)

I tell this story for several reasons. God had prophets then, and He still has prophets today. They have power with God and we should pay attention to them. We should only judge their credibility by the Word of God, being careful to remember that Jesus said, "Beware of false prophets, who come to you in sheep's clothing but inwardly they are ravenous wolves." (Matt. 7:15-NKJV)

Prophets then and now, often are not the norm. John the Baptist, first cousin to Jesus, was in the wilderness eating honey and locusts. (That in itself is rather abnormal, wouldn't you say?) King Herod of Israel had him beheaded because John boldly spoke the truth to him about his adulterous affair with his brother's wife. (Hmmm, politically incorrect, I'd assume). Many prophets in the Old and New Testament era were hated, condemned, tortured and killed because they spoke out unapologetically about sin.

As a side note, in our world today, many Christians are maligned, slandered, shunned, shamed and dubbed 'judgmental and religious fanatics' if we dare speak of sin or appear too religious.

Now Naaman would have preferred the clean waters of Damascus, as I'm sure we would have. However, sometimes God calls us to simply obey Him. The Bible says that His ways are not our ways. His ways are higher than our ways. (Isaiah 55:8-9) And like Naaman, we may have a little too much pomp and pride. God's favor is more readily bestowed upon those who are humble and obedient.

This brings me to an amazing part of 'My Song', concerning the healing I was so desperately seeking. This week's profound journey would take me more deeply into faith than I ever could have imagined!

My lifelong friend and neighbor, Judy Burke, had a friend by the name of Coleen. Coleen, like the prophets of old, is uniquely 'not normal'. She has little monetary stability. She might be considered a 'social misfit'. She smokes like a chimney and she can be abrasive, not only with her hoarse and scratchy voice, but with her 'in your face' personality. She could be very insistent. The bottom line is, she loves Jesus with all her heart.

Coleen lived in Seattle in a low income housing development. Upon learning that I had terminal cancer, she insisted that Judy and I meet her halfway between Seattle and Newport, in Portland, on a Saturday in November. Judy was to rent a 4 or 5-star hotel (REALLY?) for the three of us. Coleen believed I would be healed as she laid hands on me and prayed for me. I didn't quite 'get' what the 5-star hotel might have to do with my healing.

I instantly agreed, although I was not very comfortable with the plan (or the prophet, for that matter) but I was desperate and grasping for straws. I was not going to let any straw slip past my grasp. I was reminded, by the Holy Spirit, of the story of Naaman.

I mentioned that Coleen had very little money. However, in the first part of that week, she sent me a huge Bible in overnight mail. I noted that the postage cost her $17. It was called The Healing Bible by Morris Cerullo; a King James Bible that had commentaries and notes all through it on all the healing scriptures.

I was honored and somewhat grateful, but I also thought she was pretty foolish to spend that kind of money because I probably had no less than a dozen Bibles in my house. Not only that, but when I took the Bible out of its postal wrapping, I swear, a literal cloud of cigarette smoke hit me in the face like a smoldering volcano and nearly overwhelmed me. I said to myself, "I'm not reading this SMOKY BIBLE. I'll read my own Bible." But the Holy Spirit quickly reminded me, again, of Naaman; he thought he was too good to dip into the dirty Jordan. I immediately opened the 'Smoky Bible' and, coughing a little, I began to read.

Among the many scriptures that promoted my healing, again, I believe Isaiah 53 was key. "He was wounded for our transgressions. He was bruised for our iniquities: the chastisement of our peace was upon Him and WITH HIS STRIPES WE ARE HEALED."

Many side notes in that Bible thoroughly encouraged me. Faith comes by hearing the word of God (Rom. 10:17), but I also believe much of my faith came from reading the side notes in that particular Bible. For instance, the side notes on the whole chapter of Isaiah 53 generated MAGNIFICENT faith in my heart for the healing that I was to experience. Although the quote is slightly long, it is definitely long on power, and I pray anyone reading this will not overlook this powerful side note by Morris Cerullo on Isaiah 53.

"HEALING AND THE ATONEMENT"

Isaiah 53 clearly teaches that bodily healing is included in the atoning work of Christ on the cross of Calvary. The Hebrew words for "griefs" and "sorrows" in verse 4 specifically mean physical affliction. Matthew 8:17 says that this Isaiah text is exemplarily fulfilled in Jesus' ministry to human needs. It is evident that the words "borne" and "carried" refer to Jesus' atoning work on the cross, because the same words are used to describe His bearing our sins in Isaiah 53:11 and 1 Peter 2:24. The only use of the word "surely" in this chapter, which is a word of emphasis, precedes this provision for our salvation and healing. These verses link the provision of both salvation and healing to the cross of Calvary, but, just as in salvation, healing must be personally appropriated.

Sin and sickness are Satan's twin evils. Salvation and healing are God's twin provisions for deliverance. Before Calvary, people were saved and healed by looking forward to the cross in faith. Afterwards, salvation and healing comes by looking back to it in faith. Disease and death entered by sin, and are penalties for iniquity, so their remedy must be found in the atonement of Christ. Jesus bore our sicknesses and carried our diseases at the same time and in the same manner that He bore your sins.

"That it might be fulfilled which was spoken by Esaias the prophet, saying, Himself took our infirmities and bare our sicknesses." (Matthew 8:17) God laid both sin and sickness on Jesus in the same atonement. Peter speaks of salvation and healing as being an accomplished fact, "Who His own self bare our sins in His own body on the tree that we, being dead to sins, should live unto righteousness: by whose stripes ye were healed." (1 Peter 2:24)

Since Jesus bore your sins, it must be God's will to save when you come to Him. Since He bore your sicknesses, it must also be His will to heal when you come to Him. The same God who forgives all your sin also heals all your diseases. "Bless the Lord, O my soul, and forget not all His benefits: Who forgives all thine iniquities". (Psalms 103:2-3) The atonement of Christ has guaranteed the believer's final perfection, but both physical and spiritual human imperfections continue. The believer continues to suffer attacks of sin and sickness. The ultimate benefits of Christ's atonement are yet to be revealed.

"Who are kept by the power of God through faith unto salvation ready to be revealed in the last time." (1 Peter 1:5) The benefits of salvation to be revealed in eternity are those of physical and spiritual perfection.

When Jesus died on the cross, did He take away your sins? Do you, as a believer, still battle against sin? The same is true of sickness. Jesus died for your sickness, but as long as you are in an imperfect world and Satan is not yet bound, you must also war against sickness.

Well, back to Coleen, the trip to Portland, and hopefully a healing miracle. Judy and I both became quite apprehensive as Saturday neared for our meeting in Portland with Coleen. On Friday, I kept my appointment with my oncologist, Dr. Kenyon, in Newport, but I could barely drag myself into his office. I was extremely tired and weak. How could I ever drive the 3 hours to Portland and spend a day and a night in a hotel with a rather strange woman that I barely knew? Dr. Kenyon answered that question for me. He ordered me immediately to the Newport Hospital for a blood transfusion. I would be there for most of the day and the night.

Judy made the call to Coleen. Our meeting with her was canceled! Not to be deterred, Coleen immediately insisted, "That's O.K. Just get me a room at the Shilo. I'll come to Newport."

"The Shilo," I thought. "First she wants a 5-star hotel in Portland, and now she wants to stay at one of the better hotels in Newport. Couldn't we just put her up in a Motel 6?"

Well, there is no Motel 6 in Newport, but again I was reminded of a story in the Bible about a prophet who asked a starving widow to build him a little room in her humble home in order for him to have a place to stay. By the way, she was to make him something to eat with what little oil and flour she had left before she and her only son faced starvation.

Humbly, she agreed. Interestingly, during the drought, while others possibly died of starvation, her oil and flour never ran out. In the end, the prophet prayed for her son who had suddenly died and he was brought back to life. This story is found in 1 Kings, the 17th chapter.

Upon recalling this story, I found that the scowl on my face held a slight smile. I'm thinking that The Great Physician loves doing heart surgery.

After spending half the night in the Newport Hospital, I returned home to a fitful night of half-hoping and wondering what my meeting on Saturday would reveal with Coleen. My daughter, Kristin, had come to spend the weekend with me and I was hoping to bring her to the Shilo for our meeting with Coleen. However, Coleen demanded that only Judy and I were to be present in the room with her. Kristin had come to spend the weekend with us because early Monday morning, I was to be at the Cancer Institute in Eugene, Oregon, to begin the internal radiation treatments with Dr. Gimmel. As part of my "Team", Kristin would be there to support me.

Leaving my house Saturday evening, my feelings of expectation, hope, and yes, apprehension were palpable. Arriving at the Shilo around 7 pm, Coleen met Judy and I at the door; throwing herself in my arms, it seemed she was devoiding herself of some unseen great burden and she said, "I knew the minute I saw you and laid hands on you that you would be healed."

Even though Coleen reeked with the same smell as that Smoky Bible, I was taken aback with a true sense of hope.

Coleen proceeded to tell me that in her government run, low-income housing complex, a large black man approached her and said, "I understand you have the gift of healing. Will you pray for me?" She empathetically answered, "I will when I return from Newport where I am going to pray for a friend. I cannot let any of this healing power escape me until I have laid hands on her."

As in the account of the woman who touched the hem of Jesus' garment and was healed, I believe Coleen was experiencing some type of this heavenly virtue that Jesus spoke of, recorded in Luke 8:43-46.

The evening wore on. Judy, Coleen, and I laughed and cried. We read the Bible and prayed, sitting on her bed in the hotel room. At one point, Coleen abruptly excused herself to go outside for 'a smoke'. Upon returning to the room she said, "By the way, the cancer on your cervix is healed."

I was surprised because I had not revealed to her, nor had Judy, that the tumor on my cervix would be getting the first of many weeks of targeted radiation in just 48 hours. In fact, the medical diagnosis did not specifically mention a cervical tumor.

I couldn't wait to get home and tell Kristin and Jim all about this eventful evening. Kristin and I were especially excited. Jim was a little more calm with his expressions of excitement. As we sat on the couch recounting every detail of the evening, we picked up a devotional that I'd been given--365 Days Of Healing by Mark Brazee. Even though I may not agree with this testimony entirely, for the sake of accuracy I quote here the entire one-page devotion for November 9.

BELIEVE THE WORD, NOT THE SYMPTOMS

"For we walk by faith, not by sight."
(II Corinthians 5:7)

I heard about a lady who attended a particular church, who had a big, visible cancerous growth on her face. She'd prayed and believed she received her healing, but there was no change in her appearance. Later at a testimony service, this woman stood and said, "I want to thank God for healing me." She sat down, and people started looking at her funny. The next Sunday she stood and said, "I want to thank God for healing me." This went on for several weeks.

Some people got upset, and one person said to her, "Everyone can see you're not healed. You're causing confusion. You can't keep standing up telling people you're healed." The woman went home and stood in front of her mirror praying, "Now, Father, in Jesus' name, I know I'm healed by the stripes of Jesus. I know what the Bible says, and I know I believe it. I'd appreciate it, though, if you'd get rid of these ugly symptoms."

All of a sudden, while the woman still stood at the mirror, that big cancer just fell off and hit the floor! She looked in the mirror and saw that the area where the growth had been a moment before was covered in fresh baby skin!

You see, even though we reach out by faith and believe we receive our answer; we may not look different immediately. But we don't have to look different. We just have to believe what the Bible says, and say what we believe. Then we have what we say!

Confession

Thank God, I'm healed. No matter how I feel or what I see or what comes at me, I believe I have the victory.

This devotion would come full circle in just 48 hours when Kristin, Jim and I would go to my first internal radiation treatment with Dr. Gimmel.

68

On Monday morning, Kristin entered Dr. Gimmel's exam room with me. Dr. Gimmel tenderly and expertly inserted the microscopic instrument.

"Kristin, do you want to see the tumor?" she asked.

"Mom, do you mind?" Kristin asked.

It was kind of like, at this point, what's the difference? There was little pride left for me to deal with. I was concerned about only one thing. Dr. Gimmel clarified that the tumor was still there. What about Coleen saying the tumor was gone? I screamed silently inward. How could this be?

"See it?" Dr. Gimmel asked Kristin.

"Uh-huh. Yeah, I do see it."

Kristin hugged me reassuringly and left the room as I was put into a twilight sleep for the procedure.

I awakened and dressed, leaving the room saddened. What little faith I had was crushed to a pulp. When I climbed into the truck to leave the hospital for home, I burst into tears.

"Mom," Kristin consoled me.

"Well, what about what Coleen said this weekend, about the tumor being gone," I whined.

"Well, what about the devotion we read about the lady with the tumor on her neck? How it was there, but by faith it was gone. Have faith, Mom. I believe what Coleen said."

Kristin's words inspired me. I took a deep breath. I was determined to trust the Lord in spite of the fact that the tumor was obviously there. I knew that fact and faith often collide, and I wanted to believe that faith would come out the winner.

I was also reminded that in the Garden of Gethsemane, Jesus prayed, "Not My will, but Thy will be done."

A Second Touch

"Bring every thought captive"
(2 Cor. 10:5)

The book of Acts records the healing of a crippled man. Jesus, aware of His impending crucifixion, had told His disciples that they were to continue His ministry of healing after He was gone. " … these signs will follow those who believe … they will lay hands on the sick and they will recover." (Mark 16:17-18)

The crippled man sat begging in the town square. When Peter and Paul saw him they said to him, "Silver and gold have I none, but such as I have I give to you. In the name of Jesus Christ of Nazareth, rise up and walk!" With that, the cripple leapt to his feet and began walking and leaping and praising God.

After Dr. Kucera declared me free from cancer, cured and without a death sentence hanging over my head, I think that for the next 12 months, I went walking and leaping and praising God. It seemed that all my doctors were in awe of my healing. Dr. Garret took Dr. Kucera's place in my life of appointments for checkups. She literally glowed with joy over my remarkable health each time she examined me. Now, I religiously keep my yearly pap tests with Dr. Marcos. She smiles and comments, "You are a miracle!"

In the introduction of "My Song", I mentioned that I'd elaborate later on a miracle that Jesus performed, needing a 'second touch.' This man was born blind. Jesus made clay out of his own saliva, mixing it with dirt. Jesus applied this 'medicine' to the blind eyes. He asked the man, "How is your sight now?" The man replied, "I see men as trees walking." So Jesus reapplied the 'salve', then the man said, "Now I see clearly!" Clearly, he needed a 'second touch.'

I always stop and ponder that scene. The God-Man, Jesus—Jehovah-Rapha (The God Who Heals)--how could it be that He would miss the bull's eye on this healing? Perhaps the answer is in the 'Man' part of Jesus. The Bible says He was made like us, only without sin. He was all Man and all God. He was tempted as we all are, but He never gave into temptation (as we so often do). Perhaps He was tempted to give up and walk away, leaving the now 'partial' blind man to deal with the situation on his own. Or perhaps, Jesus does some or even many of His healing miracles in stages. The main point is that He did not give up on the blind man, but stuck with His plan to heal him.

I relate the above for a very good reason; for I, like the blind man, ended up needing another touch from the Great Physician. I faithfully kept all my appointments. The main doctor in charge of my health now was Dr. Peter Kenyon, my Oncologist.

CAT scans were scheduled every 6 months, and blood tests every three months. In August of 2010, nearly a year from the pronouncement of my healing, a CAT scan showed a suspicious lymph node near my color bone. Dr. Kenyon called me with the bad news. A PET scan was ordered, which shows greater detail than a CAT scan. I think I was more devastated than with my initial diagnosis. I just never dreamed that the cancer would return.

I'd been experiencing a dry cough, so now I began to think, "Of course, the cancer is now through my whole body. I probably have lung cancer." I believed the cancer had returned with a vengeance. The PET scan would prove that my entire lymph system would be loaded with the deadly cells. My 'doom' was predicted in my mind.

I worried about God's reputation (or was it really my own?). If I died, how would that seem to all those who'd had faith for me and had seen a true miracle?

Who would pray for all my grandkids? Especially the ones in their early twenties, when the things of the world can be so tempting? What if they needed my advice? Would they be encouraged to read from the Bible? Would anyone fast and pray and remember them before the Lord?

I would not be there for Elias, my grandson, who had a lot of personal struggles. He often came over to spend the weekend with me. We would talk and walk on the beach and sit up late. When he was depressed, I'd comfort and encourage him. He needed me! And what about my husband Jim? Who would see to it that he stayed on a healthy diet? On and on went the questions, with no answers. I thought and thought and thought. I can think a thought to death!

Jesus was friends with two sisters, Mary and Martha. They put on a big dinner party for Jesus. He sat in the living room teaching the other guests about the things of God. Mary sat at His feet, soaking in the wonderful words He spoke. Martha, however, was busy in the kitchen. She was angry that her sister was not helping. When she complained to Jesus, He said, "Martha, Martha, you are worried and troubled about so many things; but one thing is needed and Mary has chosen that good part, and it will not be taken away from her." (Luke 10:41)

Like Martha, I was worried and troubled about so many things. Jesus was saying to me, "Sande, Sande, quiet your many thoughts. Sit at My feet and learn from Me. Trust Me, and, like Mary, you will be choosing the good part that will surely benefit you and bring you peace."

I had sobbed and cried rivers of tears for 48 hours. Finally, I got ahold of myself. I should say, more accurately, the Lord finally got ahold of me. I decided, "It is what it is." I'll take whatever the PET scan reveals. I'll take it with faith, the size of a grain of mustard seed. Jesus said the mustard seed was the smallest of herbs, but if one had faith the size of a grain of mustard seed, one could remove a mountain. Here I was facing a mountain again. It had been removed once, and hopefully it would be removed again.

This brought the scriptural mandate into practice, "Casting down imaginations and every high thing that exalts itself against the knowledge of God, and bringing into captivity every thought to the obedience of Jesus Christ." (II Corinthians10:5)

What does it mean to "cast down imaginations and to bring every thought captive to Christ?" All too often, our thoughts disagree with the Word of God. A broken-hearted person may think, "I'll never be happy again." God's Word says, "He heals the broken hearted." You may think, "I have no future." God's Word says, "I have a future and a hope for you." (Jer. 29:11) Many people think, "I'm good enough to go to heaven." In contrast, the Bible says, "There is none good, no not one." Humanity needs a Savior. You might think, "I'm not smart or beautiful," but God says we are made in His image, and I don't think God is ugly or dumb.

I began dwelling, again, on the Word of God. Oh, His promises are like the Balm of Gilead--healing, soothing, Truth!

Psalm 139 tells us that God's thoughts toward us are good, and more in number than the sand. That awesome Psalm inspired me to write the words to this song:

Psalm 139
By Sande

In all of my ways, for all of my days,
I'll acknowledge Thee.
For, since my youth, and before I was born,
You have acknowledged me.
Your thoughts toward me are thoughts of peace,
They're more in number than the sand.
Well, I can't even begin to count the grains I can hold in one hand.
Such knowledge is high--it's high--it's too high for me.
You are God, the most High God--yet You pay attention to me.
When I consider the works of Your hands,
The stars, the earth, the sea …
What am I? Just who am I?
That You should be mindful of me?
You know all my ways, You count all my days,
You know when I wake, You know when I sleep.
The night shall be light, I'm in your keep
You are God--the Most High God--yet You pay attention to me.
So, in all of my ways, for all of my days,
I'll acknowledge Thee.
For since my youth and before I was born,
You have acknowledged me.

♪ ♪ ♪ ♪ ♪ ♪

Jesus began to take my thoughts captive to Himself. Again, I began to believe His Word instead of my negative thoughts. This obedience imparted peace to my troubled heart. His Word gave me courage. If I had to fight the giant again, then I would fight the giant again.

The highly anticipated phone call came from Dr. Kenyon. His name appeared on the caller ID. Taking a deep breath, I answered the phone. He wasted no time with good news--the cancer was contained in just the one lymph node. It had not spread! Breathing an audible sigh of relief, I asked, "What do we do now?"

"Now," he said, "We will aggressively target it with radiation." Optimism sounded in his voice.

This was the first week in September. I would be under radiation therapy for six weeks. The radiation treatments could not wait. Problem! Our daughter, Tanny, and her fiancé, Tyler, were to be married on October 14th, exactly six weeks from the onset of the treatments. Not only was I concerned about all the preparations for a beautiful wedding with several hundred guests, but I was to sing at the wedding. Problem! The radiologist informed me that I would lose my voice.

As I lay on that radiation table, five days a week, I prayed silently in my heavenly prayer language. I prayed that I would not lose my voice. I wanted to sing at my daughter's wedding. Jesus more than answered my prayer. Not only did I write a beautiful song, but, in honest humility, I have to say I never sang more beautifully in all my life. This is of no credit to me. All credit, glory, and honor goes to Him Who made it happen.

Remember with me the prophecy/prayer that my friend, Chris Watkins, offered when I was first diagnosed with cancer--that I would not die, for I had more songs to write and sing.

This is the song I wrote and sang for Tanny and Tyler's wedding:

I Believe in Love
By Sande

I believe in love … I believe it's true.
I believe in love … and I believe in you.
He's called us to be one … the Father, Spirit, Son …
I believe in love.
If the mountains fall into the sea and the stars should cease to shine
I will still believe in you … will you still be mine?
And if the sun forgets to rise and the moon should lose its glow,
There is something that I want you to know.
I believe in love … I believe it's true.
I believe in God and I believe in you.
He's called us to be one … the Father, Spirit, Son …
I believe in love.
If the rivers all run dry and the earth should turn to dust,
I will still believe … In God I will trust.
And when the sun is shining bright and the stars come out at night,
When the world's as it should be … and there's just you and me,
Then I believe in love … I believe it's true,
I believe in God and I believe in you.
He's called us to be one … the Father, Spirit, Son …
I BELIEVE IN LOVE.

With my daughter Tanny at her wedding.

His Word and His promises never cease to amaze me. I'm always disappointed in myself for my 'back and forth faith.' Yet, He is always faithful to me. The 11th chapter of Hebrews is called 'the faith chapter.' "Without faith it is impossible to please God, for he that comes to God must believe that He is, and that He is a rewarder of them that diligently seek Him."

He gave me the audacity to diligently seek Him. His reward to me is better than life. His reward to me is the giver of life, JESUS!

A Penny for Your Thoughts

"Are not two sparrows sold for a farthing? (penny) And not one of them is forgotten before God."
(Matthew 10:29-KJV)

I never cease to be amazed at this story. There is something about the lowly penny that God seems to honor. I think He uses the insignificant penny to prove that nothing goes unnoticed by Him. There is nothing insignificant to Him. Often, we will stoop to pick up a penny and think, "Wow! Good Luck!" The nickel, dime, quarter, etc. don't have the same slogan. Though they are more valuable, they don't seem to have the 'power punch' as the 'lucky penny'.

During my battle against cancer, my sister, Barbara, began noticing a penny here and there. Picking it up, she didn't look at it as a 'good luck' piece. She took its message to heart--"In God we trust." She was so worried about losing me to cancer. The only thing she could really do was to pray and trust. I am her only sibling. She's always been my Big Sister, being 18 months older than me, so of course she's always been watching out for me.

My one and only Sister Barbara and me.

She and her daughter, Robin, flew to Portland from San Diego to be with me during the initial scheduled operation. We had rented a house in Portland for 2 weeks so the family would have a place to stay and be close at hand. The house we rented was a tri-level 'condo' type home. Entering on the ground floor, there was just a staircase that led to the main living quarters. The bedrooms, kitchen, and living area were located up the next flight of stairs.

On the day before the surgery, I walked down the stairs to the parked car, below. There on the banister was just one small, ceramic object. Nothing else. For whatever reason, I picked it up and, to my surprise, there was a single penny that had been placed under the object. This may seem like something totally insignificant, but to me it was a Loud Clear Message--Trust in God! I need not be afraid. God was in control.

I wondered at the penny. Was it just a coincidence that I had picked up that object? Was it just a coincidence that the penny lay underneath? I didn't think so.

The next day, "Team Sande" and I arrived at Providence Hospital at 8 am sharp. The floors were sparkling clean. It seemed you could see your reflection. The first order of the day was to be weighed. The nurse took my trembling hand and helped me to step up on the scales.

I looked down and there, on the pristine floor, screaming up at me, was a shiny penny.

OK, OK, I got the message. I was to completely trust in God. And trust in God I would have to, for several hours later (as you know) the surgery was deemed unsuccessful and I was basically sent home to die.

Recovering from surgery was emotionally and spiritually draining. I received many cards of encouragement and prayers. My sister's Sorority sent me a card with an angel holding a penny. My friends, Lydi and Lori, went on a walk to talk and pray for me. They found six pennies on the ground, pasted them on a card in the form of a cross, and sent it to me.

Later that year, after I'd been declared 'cured', we had a big celebration, calling it "Sande's Life Party." The beautifully decorated tables were glittered with shiny pennies.

Today, I never see a penny, but what I stoop, pick it up and thank God for the miracle He gave me. He simply but profoundly kept reminding me to trust in Him. I believe He communicated hope and love to me by a lowly penny.

Dr. Kucera, Again

"Physician heal thyself"
(Luke 4:23)

My last appointment with Dr. Gimmel, my angel doctor, was in early January 2010. Again, I was put into a twilight sleep for the last of the internal radiation treatments. She gently shook me awake, speaking softly in my ear.

"You are cured of cervical cancer," came the softly whispered words.

Was I dreaming? The voice was as soft as an angel's. Was I awake? Had I heard correctly, or had I misunderstood? Was it really Dr. Gimmel speaking? My cloudy brain began to clear.

"You are cured of cancer," she said again. It seemed surreal, yet somehow true.

"I'm ordering you a CAT scan. When I get the report back I'll send it to Dr. Kucera, but you are cured!" Excitement echoed in her voice. "Dr. Kucera's the quarterback, so the official word will come from him."

Oh, how I hoped what she said was right. However, I would not … could not … accept the full meaning of this until I was examined by Dr. Kucera, along with his affirmation of the CAT scan results.

Jesus, Himself, healed ten lepers, but told them they must go to the priests at the Temple before they could be declared 'clean' (healed). Luke's Gospel recounts the details: "As He entered a certain village, there met Him ten men, leprous men who stood afar off. And they lifted up their voices and said, Jesus, Master, have mercy on us! And when He saw them, He said to them, 'Go and show yourselves to the priests.' And it came about that as they were going, they were cleansed. And one of them, when he was healed, returned and with a loud voice glorified God, and fell down on his face at His feet, giving Him thanks. So Jesus answered and said, 'Were there not ten lepers cleansed? But where are the nine?' And He said to him, 'Arise, go your way. Your faith has made you well.'" (Luke 17:11)

I added a new pet name to my beloved Dr. Kucera--along with Goofy, Dr. Conservative, the Liar, and Quarterback--and now, Dr. Kucera, the Priest!

I did as Dr. Gimmel prescribed. I had the CAT scan and made the appointment with Dr. Kucera. For a week, I lived in a fog until I found myself waiting for Dr. Kucera to enter the examination room. A soft knock on the door announced his arrival. For what seemed like the hundredth time, I lay looking up at the ceiling with my feet in the stirrups. I would hear him mutter, "Hmmmm ... ohhhh ... ahhhh" and finally, an uncharacteristic, enthusiastic, "WOW!" For 'Doctor, Goofy, Conservative' to be so demonstrative, I was fascinated and curious. I held my breath, hoping that he'd be agreeing with Dr. Gimmel. But I had been disappointed before.

He finished the exam, making no further comment. I was to meet him in his office where my original "Team Sande" members were anxiously waiting. I quickly dressed, opened his door and took a chair in the close-knit circle. Dr. Kucera sat in a black leather swivel chair, with his big, black shoes barely tucked under the desk. He was reading the CAT scan report off his computer. The room was heavy with silence. Slowly swiveling around to face us, he simply said,

"You don't have cancer anymore."

Being only slightly prepared for him to say this, I let his words register for a moment, and then asked,

"So when do I have the operation?"

"Yes!" my family chimed in, "When do you schedule the operation?"

He soberly responded, "Why would we operate when there is no cancer? You do not have cancer."

There was victory in his voice! It was difficult to get our minds around the truth of his words. But it was true! It was official! The 'Dr. Priest' had spoken. I was free from cancer!

"Make an appointment at the front desk and I'll see you in six months for your post cancer checkup," he said, enthusiastically. "You are free to go."

He rose from his swivel chair.

My mind was going a thousand miles a minute. I was healed! Should I tell him about the healing of the ten lepers? Should I tell him how I'd deemed him my cancer 'priest'? Would he think me a fanatic? Would I embarrass my family?

"Just a moment," I heard myself say. I reached up to put both my hands on his shoulders, insinuating that he should sit down. It seemed he was a small child humbly obeying a parent. He sat back down.

"I have something to tell you," I began. I related to him my conversation with Dr. Gimmel, how I'd have to hear from him, 'the quarterback'. I told him the whole story of the ten lepers and how I considered him 'the priest'. My voice shook with emotion and gratitude. He listened intently. Understanding registered on his face.

He took me by surprise when he dryly asked,

"Well, what did Jesus do about the nine that didn't return to thank him?" He added, "I bet He was really mad at them."

"No," I answered, "He forgave them. He loved them, and He loves you, too!" I added.

With that, Dr. Kucera gave me a huge, sincere bear hug. Wrapped in his big, long arms I said:

"When I first came in here, I didn't think I had much hope."

"Neither did I," he admitted. The room was silent with wonder. That's when I dubbed him: 'Dr. Kucera, the Liar'.

Almost six months had passed when I received a letter in the mail from Providence Hospital. I supposed it to be an affirmation of my six-month appointment with Dr. Kucera. I disregarded it as I had the date marked on my calendar.

I cannot describe my sorrow and shock when I called his office to confirm my appointment. The voice on the other end was unreal.

"Oh, I'm so sorry to tell you that Dr. Kucera died last week. Didn't you get a letter of notice that he had passed away?"

Died? Passed away? Gone? How could Dr. Goofy, Conservative, Awesome Quarterback, Priest of cancer, Wonderful Liar, Lesser Physician, die? He had helped to save my life. Without him, I wouldn't be here! Yes, he had cancer, but so what? So had I! He just couldn't have died!

I attended his memorial service in Salem, Oregon. The beautiful hall was filled with doctors, lawyers, nurses, friends, family, and patients.

When the mourners were invited to speak at an open mic, Jim nudged me and encouraged me to speak. After several nudgings, I finally approached the microphone. There was a sweet wave of gentle laughter as I re-told the story of how I'd said to him,

"I believe in miracles", and he countered with, "We doctors believe in the miracles of chemo and radiation." I responded with, "Well, I believe in the Great Physician and the lesser physician," and he asked, "And who is the Great Physician?" I answered, "That would be Jesus." "And the lesser?" he asked. "That would be you."

Later during the reception, a nurse approached me. She took me by surprise when she said, "We will see Dr. Kucera again in the Kingdom of Heaven." She began to relate an incident that involved her while she was assisting him in a surgery, which caused her to KNOW that Dr. Kucera believed in Jesus.

I like to think that I helped to save his spiritual life as he had helped to save my physical life. God's ways are surely past finding out. Apart from referring to him by all the various nametags I stuck on him, I now refer to him as "My God Given Doctor", whom I will surely see again.

I Believe

By Sande, around 1975

I believe in the sun, when the sun doesn't shine.
I believe in the stars, though I don't see them each time.
I believe in the bulb, though it's laid bare in the ground,
I believe in springtime, its bloom will be found.
In the dead of winter, with no bud on the tree,
I believe, late in summer, it will bear fruit for me.
I believe in things I cannot see,
For God uses nature to tell us of things that will be.
And I believe in the love that two people share;
I believe we'll meet again in the air.

♪ ♪ ♪ ♪ ♪ ♪

"For the Lord Himself will descend from heaven with a shout and with the voice of an arch angel and with the trumpet of God. And the dead in Christ shall rise first. Then we who are alive and remain shall be caught up together with them in the clouds to meet the Lord in the air, and thus we shall always be with the Lord. Therefore comfort one another with these words."

(I Thessalonians 4:16-18)

Jehovah-Rapha
The God Who Heals

Well, I have written much about the healing hand of God, Jesus, the Great Physician, and the prophet Isaiah's proclamation, that by His stripes we are healed. It is more than obvious that our God is a gracious, loving, and kind God that longs to bless the people of His creation.

When my niece, Robin, first learned of the challenge I was facing with cancer, she knew there would be an answer for hope in the Bible. Not being familiar with the scriptures, she decided to 'Google God.' The computer printed out the following:

"A furious squall came up, and the waves broke over the boat, so that it was nearly swamped. Jesus was in the stern, sleeping on a cushion. The disciples woke him and said to him, 'Teacher, don't you care if we drown?' He got up, rebuked the wind and said to the waves, 'Quiet, be still.' Then the wind died down and it was completely calm. He said to his disciples, 'Why are you so afraid? Do you still have no faith?' They were terrified and asked each other, 'Who is this? Even the wind and the waves obey him.'" (Mark 4:37-41)

And, "Praise the Lord, O my soul, all my inmost being, praise thy holy name. Praise the Lord, O my soul, and forget not all his benefits, who forgives all your sins and heals all of your diseases, who redeems your life from the pit and crowns you with love and compassion." (Psalm 103:1-4)

If you are searching for answers, as Robin was, and you're not sure what God is saying, then, like Robin, just 'Google God.'

Two of my friends, Velma, and Beth, living in different states and not acquainted with each other, sent me the same scripture. That scripture spoke of my enemy (cancer), which would be as 'a nonexistent thing'. How beautifully that came to pass in my life!

I so love this beautiful poem, depicting the God Who became a man and was prophesied 700 years before His birth, that He would be wounded for our transgressions, and that we would be healed by His stripes. (Isaiah 53)

Isaiah 53
By Edward Shillito

The other gods were strong, but Thou was weak
They rode, but Thou didst stumble to a throne;
But to our wounds, only God's wounds can speak
And not a god has wounds but Thou alone.

In Robin Roberts' interview with Ladies Home Journal in the August 2008 issue on her battle with cancer, she was asked, "What role has your faith played in all of this, Robin?" Many questions and answers were involved in that conversation.

She ended the interview with this, "But I will say this, to know people of all faiths, whether it was in a church, or a temple or a mosque, were lifting me up, praying on my behalf. You cannot not be a changed person, knowing so many different people around the world were lifting you up to their respective god, that's powerful and it's going to stay with me."

While I appreciate her comments and candid observations, I cannot give credit to any 'respective god'. The Bible clearly says that there are many gods, but only One True and Living God--Jehovah. He alone is Jehovah-Rapha, The God Who Heals.

The Word of God is quick and powerful and sharper than any two-edged sword. Do you need hope? Do you need help? Do you need healing? Do you need forgiveness? It's all in the Book. The Book of Life. The B I B L E.

Heaven

"Surely this is the gate of heaven"
(Genesis 28:17)

Heaven ... What is it? ... Where is it? ... Who will go there? ... How do we get there? We all want to go there ... eventually ... but not just yet. We certainly do not want to take the only vehicle that gets us there ... Death. What a predicament! The Bible declares that the last enemy to be destroyed is death. (1 Cor. 15:26)

The main character in the popular series of novels, No. 1 Ladies Detective Agency, written by Alexander McCall Smith, is a heavy-set African woman who resides in Botswana, Mma Ramotswe. In number 2 of the series, she has agreed to marry Mr. J.L.B. Matekoni. Her problem is which house to live in once they are married. I quote her dilemma in this section of the book, pages 7 and 8.

"Her house on Zebra Drive had many good qualities, but it was rather close to the center of town and there was a case for being farther away. His house, near the old airfield, had a larger yard and was undoubtedly quieter, but was not far from the prison and was there not an overgrown graveyard nearby? That was a major factor. If she were alone in the house at night for any reason, it would not do to be too close to a graveyard. Not that Mma Ramotswe was superstitious. Her theology was conventional and had little room for unquiet spirits and the like, and yet, and yet ..."

"In Mma Ramotswe's view there was a God, Modino, who lived in the sky, more or less directly above Africa. God was extremely understanding, particularly of people like herself, but to break his rules, as so many people did with complete disregard, was to invite retribution. When they died, good people, such as Mma Ramotswe's father, Obed Ramotswe, were undoubtedly welcomed by God. The fate of the others was unclear, but they were sent to some terrible place-- perhaps a bit like Nigeria, she thought--and when they acknowledged their wrong doing they would be forgiven."

Unlike Mma Ramotswe's ideas of heaven and God, as sweet, endearingly naive as they are, the Bible tells a different story. We learn from the Bible that there were two destinies after death. There was a great gulf fixed between the two places. One was a place of torment, the other a place of comfort. (Luke 16:19-31) After Jesus was crucified, the place of comfort was re-located to a place called heaven. (Ephesians 4:8-10)

The place of torment must still be located in its original setting. Since Jesus paid for all our sins on the cross, we who believe are immediately ushered into the presence of the Lord, the moment we die. "To be absent from the body is to be present with the Lord." (2 Corinthians 5:8)

Jesus tells the true story of His friend, Lazarus. Lazarus had died. When Jesus arrived on the scene of the mourners, He had a conversation with Lazarus' two sisters, Mary and Martha. Martha said to Jesus, "Lord if you had been here my brother would not have died." (John 11:21) Jesus said to her, "Your brother will rise again." (John 11:23) "I am the resurrection and the life. He who believes in Me, though he may die, he shall live. And whoever lives and believes in Me shall never die." Then He really pushes the issue and point blank asks her, "Do you believe this?" (John 11:25-26)

And we must ask ourselves, do we believe this? Do we believe in Jesus? Do we believe what He did for us and what He says to us? Acts 16:31 says, "Believe on the Lord Jesus Christ and you shall be saved." Perhaps it seems oversimplified, but the word 'believe' in the original Greek language means to trust in, rely on, and cling to. Believing in Jesus is to trust in what He's done for us on the cross, and to rely on Him for our salvation. We are to cling to Him in times of trouble and times of wellbeing.

Jesus said, "If you love Me, then keep my commandments." We think, "Oh no: the Big Ten. Impossible! I've tried."
But Jesus knows that we CANNOT keep the Ten Commandments. That's why He kept them for us. Jesus takes us to the heart of the matter, or I should say He takes us to the matter of the heart. Jesus said there are only two laws to keep, and that is to love God, and to love your neighbor. Love works no ill toward God or toward our neighbor. In another place one of the disciples asked Jesus, "What must we do to do the works of God?" They might've been thinking things like, go to the synagogue every day, kneel three times a day toward Jerusalem, ride a camel around the desert and preach to all the Nomads, or give all you have to the poor, but Jesus answered them, saying, "This is the work of God that you BELIEVE in Him whom He has sent." (John 6:28-29)

We have been told that the streets of heaven are of pure gold, the gates are made of pearl, and the foundation is of many precious gems. There is no pain, tears, or suffering there. (Revelation 21)
While recuperating from the unsuccessful cancer surgery, I, of course, turned my thoughts toward heaven often. Now, heaven was not just someplace to believe in, but heaven was literally looming before me as my soon-to-be home. I didn't want to leave my earthly home, and I certainly did not want to leave my earthly body.
Since heaven is so wonderful and is the destiny of every believing

Christian, my question still remains: why are we so reluctant to go there?

I think part of the answer, to my satisfaction at least, is this: Genesis tells us that we are made of the earth. We are made for the earth. There is a day coming when we will reign with Christ on Earth for a thousand years, and after this there will be a new Heaven and a new Earth, which will be eternal. So I do believe we are rather earth-bound. You might say earth is just built in us!

When my cancer operation proved unsuccessful, it seemed I was being sent home to die. The Bible says it is appointed unto man once to die, and after death, the judgment. It seems paradoxical. However, as mentioned before, Jesus was judged for our sin on the cross. We are free to go to heaven. Think of that!!!! We are not sent home (to heaven) to die! We are sent home to heaven to live. TO LIVE FOREVER!

Jesus speaks to His disciples, and to us, concerning this place called heaven. John records His words, "Let not your heart be troubled; you believe in God, believe also in Me. In my Father's house are many mansions; if it were not so I would have told you. I go to prepare a place for you. And if I go and prepare a place for you, I will come again and receive you to Myself; that where I am, there you may be also." (John 14:1-3)

One of my very favorite scriptures is, "Eye has not seen, nor ear heard, neither have entered into the heart of man the things which God has prepared for those who love Him." (1 Cor. 2:9)

Listen to this magnificent description of the heavenly city that comes down to dwell on earth, taken from the book of Revelation and translated to help us understand.

The Heavenly City—The New Jerusalem

The city measures 12,000 furlongs. The length and the breadth and the height are equal. There are 8 furlongs to a mile. That means that the height, length, and breadth of the city are 1,500 miles each way. This city has 12 foundations or floors. Each foundation or floor or level bears the name of one of the 12 apostles. It is hard to comprehend just how immense the heavenly city really is.

Here are a few figures to give you a slight estimate of its magnitude. Were that city divided into rooms one mile in length and one mile high and one mile wide, it would contain 3,375,000,000 rooms, each room containing the space of one cubic mile. One of the most ASTONISHING features about such a place is the time it would require to visit or go over that city, visiting each room separately. If we were to begin at the creation of Adam and go through that city, spending one hour in each room for 24 hours a day, at the end of 6,000 years we would have visited only 52,579,580 rooms, leaving 3,344,529,440 rooms yet unvisited. Calculated in this are all the leap years that occur in 6,000 years, deducting the century year when there is no leap year.

WHAT A CITY! No mortal mind can comprehend or describe in human language … the splendor of that city. The jasper stone, clear as crystal, the sapphire, emeralds, topaz, beryl, and all the precious stones in their most glorious description are but faint comparisons when taken in relation to the glory of the city that is to come. The wall of the city is of jasper; the city itself is of pure gold. No wonder John describes it as a "bride adorned for her husband." But that is just the city. We are told that there are gates (each gate is made of pearl) on the east, north, west, and south so that God's people will have perfect liberty to examine the wonders of His universe, and God's promise to us is that He will continually show unto us the exceeding riches of His grace in His kindness towards us through Jesus Christ our Lord.

And we will have access to this magnificent place.

Ending

I will end *My Song* on this note:

"There's a time to be born and there's a time to die" (Ecclesiastes 3:1)

The answer, my friend, is not blowing in the wind ...

The answer is to SING YOUR SONG FOR HIM.

Yesterday
By Sande Schones

Yesterday I cried tears
For broken dreams and wasted years.
But today I have a song
To you I now belong.

You are my life
Through you I live
You are my gift
Through you I give

You are a tree of life to me
Through you I live abundantly

You are my Lord
You are my King

YOU ARE MY SONG, THE SONG I SING

Acknowledgements

When reading a book, I usually skip through the acknowledgements thinking …"I don't know these people anyway", but I hope in this case you will read them.

I wish to acknowledge all of my wonderful friends, family, and doctors in my healing journey of cancer. I cannot name them all and if I have left you out it is simply because my "chemo brain" has left you out. You certainly are not forgotten before God for all your prayers and hope and faith and well wishes on my behalf.

The Webster's dictionary defines "friend" as … " to love, one attached to another by affection or esteem, acquaintance, one not hostile (I like that one), one showing a kindly interest and good will, comforting, cheerful, etc".

The book of Proverbs (written by Solomon, Son of David, declared to be the wisest man who ever lived, other than Jesus himself) says this: "A friend loves at all times".

Jesus is recorded as having said this in John 15:12-15, "This is my commandment, That you love one another, as I have loved you. Greater love has no man than this, that a man lay down his life for his friends."

I can certainly say that my friends and family have fulfilled the words and commands of Jesus in loving me … praying for me … believing and hoping against hope for me when my own faith was, at first, shattered into a million pieces. They picked up the shards and made a beautiful mosaic of faith, hope, and love.

I acknowledge all the Doctors on my team: Dr. Paul Kucera, Dr.

Peter Kenyon, Dr. Fry, Dr. Gimmel, Dr. Garret, Dr. Marcos, and Dr. Paul Schones.

I give thanks to God for my wonderful family, who are my very best friends! Janet, my oldest daughter and next door neighbor, and her husband Brian (who cooked dinner for me nearly every night for 6 months), and their daughters: Ashley, Savanah, and Riley. Our one and only son Michael, and his wife Cheryl, who is not just my daughter-in-law, but a best friend. Their kids: Madison, Megan, and Mikey. Kristin, our middle daughter, and her husband Billy, and her son's Beaux and Elias. And Sandra Dawn, our youngest daughter and her husband Tyler. My one and only sister Barbara and her family in California. All my sister's in law: Roberta, Dodie, Melody, Jan, Linda and Kaye, and my friend and niece Amy Schones.

I give thanks for my wonderful family and
beautiful grandkids.

My wonderful bible study group that meets at Lisa Woodard's house and Barb Wright, the leader of Young Life. She loves every teenager she meets and though I'm not a teenager she loves me too.

My dear life long friends Denny and Judy Burke. Denny is the brother I never had and my Vietnam war hero. Tom and Linda Johnson who lost their own daughter to cancer, but hoped they would not lose me. My two Kansas childhood friends, Sondra Crusha and Madie DeSantis. My California girlfriends Beth Duboise and Joyce Dalton. My friend Kathy Sanders, who is herself a cancer survivor. My lifelong friend Joan Jones and her daughters who prayed daily for me. Lydi Johnson my "tooth fairy" who works at Dr. Palmer's office. My friend Rhonda Hamstreet who was so faithful to care about me, sending cards and her fabulous rhubarb pies. And Cindy Lockman who gave me a watch with mustard seeds in it to remind me that faith only needs to be the size of that small seed.

My sister and me with our Mother.

My lifelong friend Joan Jones visiting Jim and me in the desert.

All my pastors from Newport Four Square church and all the churches in our community along with my own church family at South Beach Church.

My best Friend and beloved husband Jim, who tirelessly drove me for chemo and radiation treatments in Corvallis, Eugene, and Portland almost every day for six months. Who cared, prayed and encouraged me and never left my side. Thank you for the wonderful life and family you have given me.

My best Friend and beloved husband Jim.

Jim and I in Reno at Hot August nights
with one of our classic cars

And last but not least, My beautiful mother, Dorothy, who prayed and hoped for me. She beat me to heaven's gate by arriving there on January 23, 2010. Cancer took her, but Jesus took cancer from her and she waits there for me.

I thank you, thank you, thank you all … Those mentioned and those not mentioned. God knows who you are and I know He will richly reward each and every one of you.

I received such an outpouring of love and
support from my friends and family.